Materials Science
WOOD
AND PAPER

making use of the secrets of matter

-◆- *Atlantic Europe Publishing*

First published in 2003 by
Atlantic Europe Publishing Company Ltd.

Author
Brian Knapp, BSc, PhD

Art Director
Duncan McCrae, BSc

Senior Designer
Adele Humphries, BA, PGCE

Editors
Mary Sanders, BSc, and Gillian Gatehouse

Illustrations
David Woodroffe

Design and production
EARTHSCAPE EDITIONS

Scanning and retouching
Global Graphics sro, Czech Republic

Print
LEGO SpA, Italy

Materials Science – Volume 3: Wood and paper
A CIP record for this book is available from the British Library

ISBN 1 86214 317 X

Acknowledgments
The publishers would like to thank the following for their kind
help and advice: *Guthrie Plantation & Agricultural Sdn Bhd and
the Kampulan Guthrie Estate*; *Peter and Ellie Nalle*; *Steve Rockell*;
Soandro; *Wing King Tong Co., Ltd.*

Picture credits
All photographs are from the Earthscape Editions photolibrary
except the following: (c=center t=top b=bottom l=left r=right)

The Pacific Lumber Company 31c; by permission of the *Syndics
of Cambridge University Library* 4/5t.

*This product is manufactured from sustainable managed forests.
For every tree cut down, at least one more is planted.*

Contents

1: Introduction   4
The value of wood   4
Wood as a practical material   6
Wood as a decorative material   9

2: What is wood?   10
Wood is made of cells   10
The parts of a tree   13
Kinds of wood   16
Cutting a tree for its grain   18
Knots   18

3: Properties of wood   19
Wood density   20
Changes in size and density with water   22
The strength of wood   24
Insulating and flame-resisting properties of wood   27
Wood and electricity   28
Wood and sound   29

4: Processing the trees   30
Harvesting and transportation   30
Tree products   32
Processing wood for special products   42

5: Paper   46
How paper is made   46
The stages of papermaking from wood   51
Types of finished paper   55
Recycling paper   56

Set glossary   58

Set index   65

(*Left*) This decorative paper has been made by pressing pieces of flower onto the wet paper surface during manufacturing.

1: Introduction

WOOD. One of the world's oldest natural materials and showing no signs of being in less demand today than it was in the past despite the huge range of competing materials that are all around us.

To understand why wood has remained a favorite material through the ages, we have to look at its properties and see how varied and useful they are. But we also have to realize that wood is not just a useful material but also a decorative one.

The value of wood

Wood has been used as a material since earliest times. It is relatively soft and easy to work. It can be a source of chemicals as well as of timber and fiber for paper. It is found in almost all parts of the world (except for deserts and polar wastes), and it is, above all, renewable (trees can be grown to replace those cut down). That is what sets it apart from many other resources that we use, such as metal, coal, and oil.

(*Below*) Many types of dwelling were produced by native Americans, each adapted to the needs of the local community. In this forest house pliable branches were bent over to form a frame and then covered with BARK to make a waterproof and largely windproof covering. Finally, the bark was held in place by a net of thin branches.

(*Left*) The ease of use of wood is vividly shown in the first pioneer cabins built by new settlers as they claimed land in the American heartland. Logs were felled and interlinked to make a frame. The wind was kept out by stuffing any gaps with soil, and the roof was finished off with turf, or sod.

Wood was first used as a simple tool. A broken branch, for example, can be used to scrape at the soil and made into a primitive plow, or it can pry up a rock and move it. Wood can also be made into a simple shelter. But it was quickly realized that wood was far more important than this—it could also be a source of fuel and so provide light and heat for warmth and cooking.

Wood has been such an important resource that in many places it has been almost used up. For example, in the 18th century the British nearly had to stop building ships for their navy because they had run out of oak trees. Even today, when so many other materials are available,

(*Above and below*) Historically, for example, in Europe wood was used for frames of buildings, with the spaces in-filled with mud, brick, or plaster.

(*Left*) The floor of a room can be clad in wood, ceiling beams can be left exposed, and wooden furniture used extensively. Together they make a room feel cosy and comfortable.

(*Left and above*) Museums such as this one in Hawaii now recreate the old ways of working with wood using simple tools. A tree trunk is crafted into a seafaring canoe.

the demand for wood is greater than ever, and the number of countries where wood is in real shortage is greater than ever. For example, countries in tropical Africa have used up so much of their wood they are forced to use dung for fuel.

Wood as a practical material

Wood is not just one material. When you look at a tree, you soon realize that the properties of leaves, branches, BARK, and TRUNK are all different. The leaves and branches are soft and pliable, and can be snapped off and used with no tools at all. The bark is a bit more tricky to pry from the trunk, but even a stone hand ax will do the job. As a result, a tree can yield many materials that are soft and readily used. Although the bulk of the wood is harder and takes more effort, nonetheless, a stone hand ax will, in time, both fell a tree and cut it into pieces.

Contrast the ease of using wood with using metal, which can only be extracted from rocks with a hot fire, and plastic, which can only be made in a chemical factory, and it is easy to see why wood has traditionally been made into everything from homes and boats to spears and plates for the table.

See **Vol. 2: Metals** *for more on the origins of metal.*

See **Vol. 1: Plastics** *for more on the origins of plastics.*

(*Below*) Wood can be made into the frame, siding, and decoration of a building, as shown here in this city historic district.

(*Right*) A piano made with wood for its decorative as well as for its sound properties.

Early peoples kept on the move, looking for fresh food. So they wanted simple and temporary shelters. As a result, the first houses were made of easily obtained materials such as twigs, leaves, and bark.

Over the centuries people began to live more settled lives, and so they changed to using materials that were longer lasting and more substantial. For this they needed materials that were strong enough to span across substantial distances. As a result, branches were replaced by logs or sawn timber, and bark on roofs was replaced by wooden tiles (often called shingles).

Even today, when a great number of materials are available for building, wood is still the most common material in places where timber is plentiful, such as the United States and Scandinavia. That is because wood still has the advantages it has always had: It is easy to cut and shape with readily available, ordinary tools. It can be fastened with simple fasteners such as nails, screws, or an ADHESIVE. It can be finished off by sanding, and it can hold a decorative finish such as paint and polish. But wood has even more advantages. Wood is also very strong, with ELASTIC properties that make it able to resist failure. Furthermore, it does not RUST like steel, and it is not attacked by acids, alkalis, or salt water like most metals. Wood is still among the best insulating materials both for heat and sound. Last and by no means least, wood has a naturally attractive finish.

(*Above*) Wood sculpted as a religious decoration, New Zealand.

See **Vol. 6: Dyes, paints, and adhesives** *for more on wood adhesives.*

(*Above*) Beautifully grained wood carved into the shape of an animal and used purely for decorative purposes.

(*Right*) African tribal sculpture.

Wood as a decorative material

One of the great advantages of wood is that it can be shaped easily. That has allowed people since earliest times to express themselves by carving in wood.

You can find wood art in every early culture across the world, and wood continues to be a favorite sculptural material today. Even in everyday uses much wood is chosen not just for its practical value but also for its beauty, especially its GRAIN. Indeed, because well-grained wood is so valuable, it is sliced up into thin sheets called VENEERS and glued over the surfaces of less attractive wood.

(*Below*) Wood sculpted into a coat of arms.

2: What is wood?

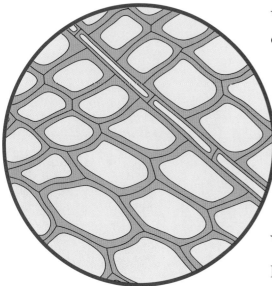

Wood is the most common natural living material on Earth. There is more living matter in the world's forests than anywhere else. Wood makes up most of the tissues of these trees and also of the shrubs that grow beneath them and of those that grow in places where it is too dry or cold for trees.

Wood is the part of the trunk, branches, and roots that strengthen the tree or shrub. The outer part of the wood also provides a place for water to move between roots and leaves.

Wood is made of cells

If you were to look at wood under a very high-powered (electron) microscope, you would see that the wood is made of CELLS. A cubic meter of wood may have half a billion or more cells.

The walls of the cells are made of a material called CELLULOSE. Cellulose makes up as much as 45% of the wood. Cellulose is, in turn, made up of very long chains of a sugar molecule called glucose.

Unlike table sugar, cellulose will not dissolve in water. However, the long chains of molecules (which make it a material called a POLYMER) allow the wood to flex, for example, in a gale.

The chains of glucose molecules are encrusted with other materials, one of the most important of which is called LIGNIN. Lignin can make up as much as 35% of the wood. Lignin gives strength to the cell walls but is not made of chains. We will see later that it is often important to separate these two types of material.

Wood also contains a range of other bonding materials. GUMS, fats, RESINS, WAXES, oils, STARCHES, and TANNINS are found inside and between the cells. These materials do not make up the fabric of the wood and can be dissolved out without altering the strength of the wood.

(*Above and below*) Almost all of the wood cells in a living tree are dead. The contents have disintegrated, but their rigid walls remain around an empty center. The exceptions are just a few rows of young cells next to the CAMBIUM (see page 12) that are produced as the tree grows and a few cells (called parenchyma cells) in the SAPWOOD.

The walls of each cell are made from a tough material called cellulose and also contain lignin. They protect the softer material of the cell while the cell is alive and provide the framework of support once it has died.

(Below) Redwood trunks, northern California. They are softwood trees. When a tree is felled, a huge bulk of material is available to work with. Notice, however, that the wood is not perfect, and so careful cutting is needed to get as much good wood as possible from the trunks. To prevent waste, the remaining wood will have to be processed into chips or paper.

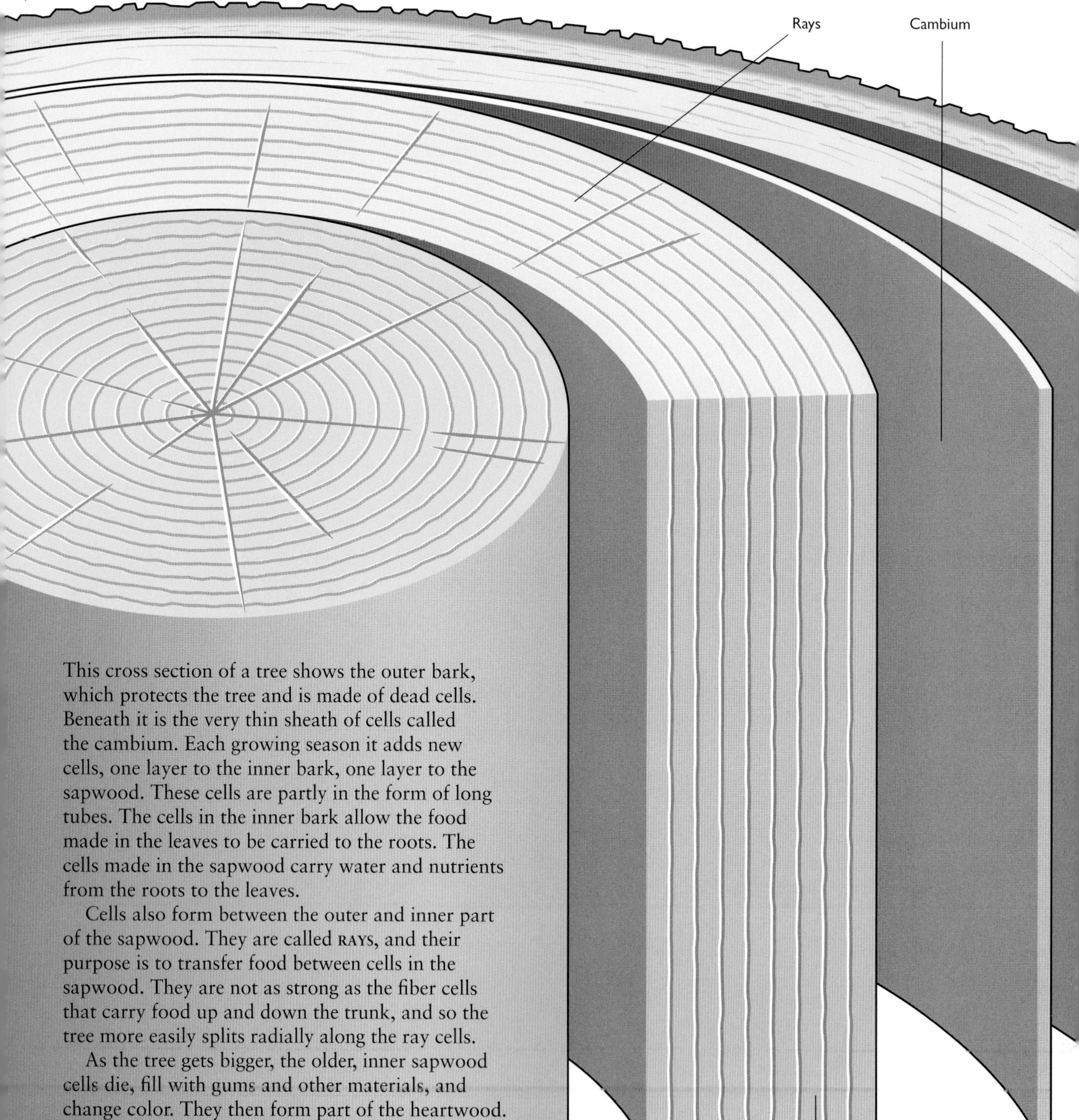

Rays   Cambium

This cross section of a tree shows the outer bark, which protects the tree and is made of dead cells. Beneath it is the very thin sheath of cells called the cambium. Each growing season it adds new cells, one layer to the inner bark, one layer to the sapwood. These cells are partly in the form of long tubes. The cells in the inner bark allow the food made in the leaves to be carried to the roots. The cells made in the sapwood carry water and nutrients from the roots to the leaves.

Cells also form between the outer and inner part of the sapwood. They are called RAYS, and their purpose is to transfer food between cells in the sapwood. They are not as strong as the fiber cells that carry food up and down the trunk, and so the tree more easily splits radially along the ray cells.

As the tree gets bigger, the older, inner sapwood cells die, fill with gums and other materials, and change color. They then form part of the heartwood. The heartwood helps provide strength to the tree and also stores water for the living sapwood, although it is not essential in holding the tree up. That is shown by many old standing trees whose heartwood has rotted away.

Sapwood

Heartwood

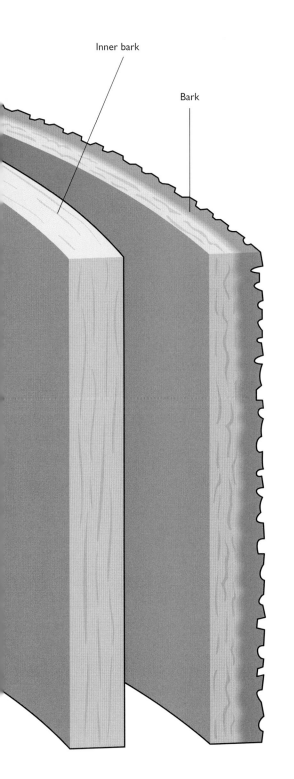

Inner bark

Bark

Most of the cells in wood are dead, even though the trees are living. The dead cells are to be found near the center of the stem or root and are blocked with resins and gums.

The parts of a tree

If you cut a stem (trunk or branch) or a root of a tree, you will always find that it contains four different zones.

In the center is the region called the PITH, also called the HEARTWOOD. The new, or sapwood, grows around the pith, and in places with marked temperature seasons it adds a layer each growing season. As a result, many pieces of wood show a series of concentric rings. All of these rings are dead except for the outermost.

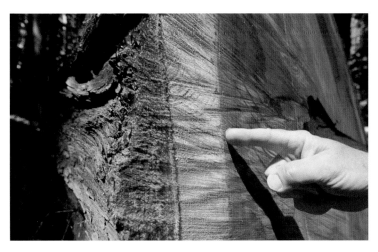

(*Above*) The junction between the darker heartwood and the lighter sapwood in a cross section of a redwood trunk.

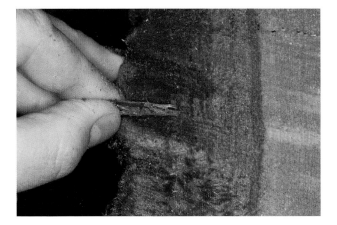

(*Right*) A detail of the thick, fibrous protective bark on the outer edge of a redwood trunk. The growing cambium layer is only a few cells across and so cannot be seen with the naked eye, but it occurs at the junction of the bark and the sapwood.

(*Below*) Rays, the radiating lines that show up in a cross section, mark the bands of cells that transfer food and water across the living part of the trunk.

The inner part of the wood, the heartwood, is much darker than the outer part, known as the sapwood. The heartwood is made of tissue that is now dead, while the sapwood still contains live tubelike cells that carry water (as sap) from the roots to the leaves and also store food. Outside these wood layers is a thin layer of living cells that is responsible for the future growth. This layer, which is so thin that it cannot be seen with the naked eye, is called the cambium. And beyond the cambium lies the final part, the bark. Each year the cambium adds between 10 and 20 times as much thickness to the sapwood as it does to the bark.

It is often possible to see lines, called RAYS, radiating from the center to the outer parts of the wood. They are the cells that transfer food between the inner and outer parts of the sapwood. They also extend into the heartwood because it was formerly sapwood. These cells are not as strong as other cells, and so the trunk most easily splits along its rays.

As a plant ages, resins and other materials flow toward the center along the rays. The resins and gums then fill up the cells close to the center of the tree, making it harder and denser. That is how sapwood changes to heartwood.

Some softwood trees have cells that contain enough resin for it to ooze out when the wood is cut.

The growth rings visible in a cross section of a tree trunk growing in a seasonal climate are not uniform. Instead, each ring consists of an inner, thicker part called the EARLY WOOD or springwood and a thinner outer part called the LATE WOOD or summerwood. The early wood is added at the start of the growing season when the plant is developing most vigorously. It has bigger, more open cells than the late wood, which forms when the main thrust of growing is past. The early wood is less dense and slightly softer than the late wood.

(*Below and right*) The trunk and section of an aspen. Rays are almost invisible.

(*Above and left*) The trunk and section of a eucalyptus. Rays are very marked.

(Above and below) Examples of the difference in appearance of a white pine when cut in two different directions and showing different grain patterns. White pine is a softwood.

Kinds of wood

Each kind of tree produces its own characteristic kind of wood. However, trees can be broadly classified into just two groups: SOFTWOODS and HARDWOODS.

Softwood

Softwood is the name for timber that comes from a coniferous (cone-bearing) tree. The main conifers are pine, spruce, fir, cedar, and redwood. In fact, the word does not really refer to the softness of the wood—even though many softwoods are indeed soft—since some softwoods, for example, yew, are hard.

Softwoods are used for about four-fifths of the world's building timber. They mainly grow either in cooler regions or warm, dry parts of the world.

(Below) This is a section through the trunk of a softwood tree. Notice the widely spaced rings and the "coarse" grain. They are produced by the large wood cells and rapid growth associated with most softwoods.

(Below) The grain of another softwood tree, a Douglas fir.

(Right) The grain of a yew, showing why it is a popular tree when decorative wood is needed. Yew is a very hard softwood.

Hardwood

Hardwood is the name for timber from flowering trees—those with broad leaves. Many broad-leaved trees are found in the midlatitudes and the tropics, especially those areas with rainfall throughout much of the year.

Many hardwoods grow much more slowly than softwoods, and so their wood is more dense than softwoods. Trees such as oak and beech are typical hardwoods of the midlatitudes, while teak is a hardwood from tropical forests. Some hardwoods, for example, balsa, are softer than softwoods. The grain of many hardwoods makes them prized for quality furniture.

(Below) The grain of a poplar—a hardwood tree.

Cutting a tree for its grain

The direction of the wood fibers is known as the grain. Most fibers are arranged in the long direction of the stem or root. There are also cells that make up the rays and others that run across the wood. As a result, cutting across a stem cuts through the long cells and shows rays as lines like spokes in a wheel. Cutting lengthwise cuts with the long grain and sometimes shows the rays as bands of cells. Thus by cutting the wood in various ways, combinations of these cells can be revealed. That is what gives the wood its different types of grain. Careful selection of grains produces the best-looking veneers.

(Above) The grain of a red oak (a hardwood).

(Right) The grain of a piece of beech (a hardwood) cut lengthways.

Knots

The normal pattern of the grain is often interrupted by irregularities. The most common among them are KNOTS.

Knots are circular patterns of grain that are common in trees. Each knot represents a place, or node, from which a branch has grown. Knots are usually very hard and difficult to cut, and quite often the part of the grain belonging to the branch (the knot itself) falls out when the wood is cut. Knots occur largely in the surface parts of the sapwood and do not affect the interior. Knotty parts of trees are usually unsuitable for many construction or decorative purposes.

(Left) Knots in timber. Knots mark places where branches join the main stem.

3: Properties of wood

Wood has many desirable properties. Not only does it show an attractive finish, but it has great strength when put under load, when put under tension, or when twisted. It is naturally perfectly elastic, which means that it will go back to its starting position once a force is removed. Wood is, however, not PLASTIC, that is, it will not change shape permanently when a load is applied. In this respect it is both PLIABLE (because it is very elastic) and BRITTLE (because it will snap when overstressed).

Over time wood will shrink and change shape. Changing shape is called warping and is a natural feature seen in all old furniture. Warping can be reduced by care in construction. As a result, much old furniture shows no signs of warping, but a cheaply made door might warp in a few months.

(Above) The natural variability of wood can be used to great effect, as in these oak floor blocks.

(Below) Hardwood can be cut to make fine edges. It is also durable and attractive, as this teak garden furniture shows.

Woods are remarkably varied to look at. Some woods have knots; others have SHAKES, CHECKS, and so on. Shakes and checks are splits, while knots are places where branches joined. Shakes, where the rings split apart, are usually the result of bacterial infection. All of these features are seen as "defects" from the wood-user's point of view and make the wood weaker and less useful in places where appearance or strength are important.

Wood density

The density of wood varies considerably between species of tree. The least dense (like balsa) have a density of about 0.1 grams per cubic centimeter, while more dense woods such as the Douglas fir are 0.45 grams per cubic centimeter. The densest woods (such as ironwood) have densities of up to 1.2 grams per cubic centimeter and will blunt a saw.

Because the density of water is 1.0 grams per cubic centimeter, the densest wood sinks. On the other hand, the lightest wood floats very high in the water, while wood of medium density floats about halfway in the water.

The difference in density between woods comes from the amount of materials such as gums and resins and from the thickness of the wood cell walls. Varying density affects the way a wood is used. For example, a dense, heavy wood is unlikely to be used in interior

(Above and below) Cracks that are parallel to the rings are called shakes, while cracks that are radial are called checks.

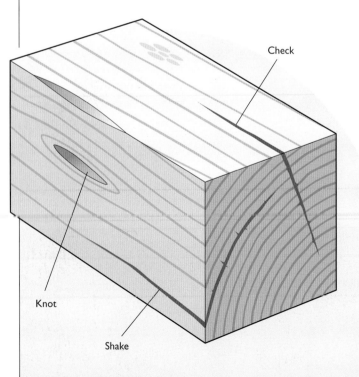

Check

Knot

Shake

(Right) Decorative and functional wood, as in this bench, requires strong timber that is nice to look at. As a result, it must be free from knots and resistant to warping. Cheaper benches often use uncured wood of inferior quality to save money. That is why the slats on cheap benches warp after they have been out in the open for a few weeks.

construction because it is harder to cut and heavier, although it may well be used as siding because of the superior rot-resisting properties given to it by the thicker gum- and resin-encrusted cells.

Changes in size and density with water

All of the cells in wood are able to soak up water, so that a piece of wood swells and gets heavier when it gets wet and shrinks and gets lighter as it dries out.

As a wood gets wetter, it becomes softer. The fibers are also less easy to cut, and they tend to tear. Wood is also weaker when it is wet compared to when it is dry. However, wet wood will bend more easily (it is more pliable) than dry wood. Thus a twig with sap rising is much less likely to snap than a dry one. Similarly, a steam-heated piece of wood is easier to bend into furniture than a dry one.

Because wood soaks up moisture, its density is always changing. As it becomes wetter, the hollow insides of the cells fill up and add weight. However,

(Above) It is easier to carve precise shapes in denser woods such as this tropical hardwood.

when water is soaked up by the cell walls, they swell as well as gain weight. Normally, cell walls contain between a quarter and a third water by weight.

You can see these changes clearly in logs that are floating in water on their way to a sawmill. The logs gradually float lower and lower in the water as they soak up more water.

Some woods can hold enormous amounts of water, far greater than their dry weight. The water gets not only inside the cells but also between the cellulose chains in the cell walls. In this way wood behaves like a giant sponge. Balsa can hold up to eight times its own weight of water, pine can hold two and a half times its dry weight, and even a hardwood like beech can hold more than its own weight of water.

Because water inside the cells makes the wood heavy, when a tree is felled and left, it begins to lose water from inside the cells. That is why logs are often left for a while before being transported to the sawmill. By the time they are moved, the logs are much lighter than when the trees were felled.

Although the cells are empty and the wood is lighter, at this stage the wood has hardly shrunk. It only shrinks significantly when it continues to dry, and the water starts being shed from the cell walls.

When a piece of wood dries out, it changes size by different amounts in each direction. Its length changes by perhaps a fifth of 1%—hardly noticeable. It may lose over 4% of its wet size measured across the trunk. Overall, the total change in volume is about 12%.

This difference is very important because as wood in a building ages, provided it has been cut with the fiber grain, the length of the timbers hardly changes as it gets damp and dry in normal use.

Because the timbers used are relatively small across the fiber grain, the bigger changes in this direction are also hardly noticeable. If they were the other way around, timber would be much more awkward to use for construction because all of the timber joints would pull apart as the wood dried.

(Below) When you see piles of timber stacked for months, you may think that it has been forgotten. In fact, the owners are waiting for some of the moisture to be lost naturally and so reduce the cost of transporting it.

(Right) Because sheet timber has a tendency to warp, it is often combined in a LAMINATE with the grain of one sheet placed at right angles to the grain of the next sheet. The sheets are locked together with adhesive. This is how plywood is made.

Although wood may not shrink much in the direction of the fiber grain, that does not mean that wood dries uniformly. As many builders know, wood often dries irregularly, and that causes a distortion to the timber or sheeting known as WARPING. Warping can, however, be overcome by using suitable bracing pieces during construction. Even sawing can cause warping because it releases the stresses that were in the wood but balanced when it was whole.

The problems with warping are one reason that composite wood panels are used, of which one well-known type is PLYWOOD.

Dry wood is much more resistant to decay than wet wood. All of these reasons explain why people do their best to dry wood and then keep it dry using waterproofing such as creosote when necessary (see page 40).

Wet wood will also not take up glue, while wet fibers will not make a smooth finish.

The strength of wood

Wood has fibers running along the length of the stem or root—the grain. This pattern of fibers makes the wood much stronger along the grain than across the grain when it is pulled or compressed. However, the opposite is true when it is bent. Wood is far stronger when bent across the grain than with the grain.

The density of the wood is a good indicator of the strength of a wood. The more dense it is, the stronger it is.

Wood gets stronger as it gets drier. Wood becomes less strong as it is heated. Wood will also support much larger loads for a short time than for a long time. That explains why, for example, you can

Compression

Bending

(Left, right, and below) Wood can take greater bending loads with the grain than across it. It will also take greater compression loads across the grain and with it. Nevertheless, other considerations, such as length of timber, may be more important in determining which kind is used.

put a row of books on a bookshelf, and the shelf will stay perfectly level, but a few months later the shelf may have bowed downward.

Most importantly, strength is greatly affected by defects in the wood. For example, shakes and knots reduce strength dramatically because they represent places where the fibers of the wood no longer interlock. Because of this, wood is often graded to ensure that it will, in general, be more likely used for the correct purpose. A wood with knots or shakes is graded lower than a perfect piece of wood, the exact grade depending on the experienced eye of a lumber merchant. It is not a scientific scale, but rather a practical one.

(Above and below) The strength of wood is well illustrated by this historic grist mill. Every part of this mechanical structure is made of wood, including the gears on the gearwheel. Notice the barrels made of wood used for storing the grain. Only the hoops holding them together are metal.

Insulating and flame-resisting properties of wood

Wood has useful heat-insulating properties. That is why homes made from wood are naturally good at keeping in the heat in winter and keeping out the heat in summer. Also, because wood does not readily conduct heat away, it feels warm when touched.

Wood also expands and contracts very little as its temperature changes. That is an important property both for keeping buildings warm, cool, and draftproof, and also for preventing the spread of fires.

Wood therefore has many advantages for use in buildings, not just as structural timbers but also as insulating panels. However, the insulation properties of wood are quite different with and against the grain. Wood will conduct heat over twice as well with the grain than across the grain. By choosing to cut the wood across the grain, therefore, the wood can be used for maximum insulation.

The heat-insulating properties of wood are, in part, determined by the amount of air trapped in cells. The bigger the cells, the better the insulation properties. This means that a low-density wood, such as pine, holds more air and therefore conducts heat more slowly than a high-density wood, such as maple.

Wood conducts heat faster when it is wet than when it is dry. This is an important additional reason for keeping wood dry when it is to be used in construction.

Of course, if the temperature of the wood is raised too much, it starts to burn. Most wood begins to burn at temperatures above 400°C. At this point the inflammable gases being given off by the heated wood (from its gums and resins between and

(Above and below) Whole trunks have been made into the walls of cabins, shops, and even theaters. This method is simple and also uses the good insulating properties of the wood.

(Above) Wood makes a
warm flooring because of its
good insulating properties.
Hardwoods like oak also resist
soaking up spills and stains.

inside the cells) catch fire spontaneously. A source of flame
is not needed for wood to catch light above 400°C.

Once alight, wood has a very high CALORIFIC value,
meaning that wood will give out a lot of heat as it burns.
This is, of course, the reason for using wood as a fuel. The
release of heat is up to 5,000 kilocalories per kilogram.
But this also causes problems when one tries to put out
fires in wooden buildings. As a result, while it is sensible
to use wood for its construction and insulation properties,
it also makes sense to protect it from possible sources of
high temperature such as from open fires and in kitchens.

Wood and electricity

Dry wood is not only a good heat insulator but a very
good insulator of electricity. However, as wood soaks
up moisture in damp air, it becomes much less good as
an electrical insulator. As wood changes from very dry
to the point where the fibers are full of water (but the
cells are not), the resistance of wood goes down by ten
million fold. Between that level and full saturation the
resistance only goes down 50-fold. This is true more or
less irrespective of the kind of tree the wood comes from.
This decrease in resistance explains why wood itself is not
used as a reliable electrical insulator in exterior locations.
Instead, ceramic insulators are used between metal
electricity wires and wooden utility poles.

See **Vol. 4: Ceramics** for more on
ceramic insulators.

Wood and sound

Wood is well known in its use for musical instruments and loudspeaker cabinets. This is no accidental choice. Wood can amplify or absorb sound waves in its surroundings.

When a sound reaches wood from somewhere in the environment, it is partly absorbed and partly reflected. At the same time, the wood is set in motion, so that it also vibrates. A thin sheet of wood will vibrate more than a solid block. This combination of properties is used to amplify the sound of the strings in a violin and other string instruments, but it is also used, less obviously, in organ pipes and woodwind instruments.

The pitch of sound produced depends on the frequency of vibration and the dimensions, density, moisture content, and elasticity of the wood. The change in pitch with moisture content of the wood explains why an instrument has to be retuned each time it is used.

How is it that wood can be used to amplify sound in musical instruments and at the same time be able to absorb energy and be used as a sound-proofing partition? The key is in whether or not the wood is allowed to vibrate.

Wood would normally absorb no more than 5% of the energy striking it. But by using a combination of wood with cavities containing porous materials, the wood can absorb 90% of the sound. It is this type of construction that is often used in interior doors to muffle sound.

(Above and below) Musical instruments such as this cello and thumb harp depend on the elastic properties of wood to resonate and so amplify the vibrations produced by the strings.

4: Processing the trees

A tree is a living thing. Wood is a material. Between the two lies a complicated system of processing that determines the use of the tree and its value.

Before trees can be processed, they must be felled and transported to the sawmill. Trees are normally cut during their DORMANT season if there is one. In the case of DECIDUOUS trees this means that the sap is not rising, and the leaves are not an extra burden to cut away.

Harvesting and transportation

As soon as a tree has been harvested, it not only begins to dry out, but it is also vulnerable to a wide range of insects and fungi that feed on dead plant tissue. By harvesting in the dormant season (for example, winter), advantage can be taken of the reduced number of active insects, while the temperatures are not favorable to fungi growth.

Many places with softwood forests and heavy winter snowfall also harvest their trees in winter because the snow makes it easier to tow the felled logs from the forest stands to a collection point. In some case logs are hauled to frozen rivers, where they wait until the spring thaws. The logs then float down to the mills with very little additional transportation costs.

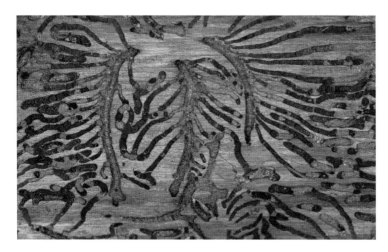

(Left and above) Wet wood is an attractive home for a multitude of insects as well as for fungi and bacteria. That is why wet wood decays much faster than dry wood. If the bark of a felled log is broken away, for example, it can be seen clearly to be the home for a range of burrowing insects. To reduce damage, the wood needs to be used. If it is to be kept outside, it has to be treated with a preservative within a reasonable time after felling.

(*Above*) Felling the timber and rough cutting to transportable lengths.

(*Above*) Gathering logs for transport by road.

(*Left*) Rapid transportation is the key to being able to make the most of forests. It was an early priority for railroads, as shown here in California. Today the logs from the same forests are mostly transported by road on trucks.

(*Below*) Floating logs to a sawmill.

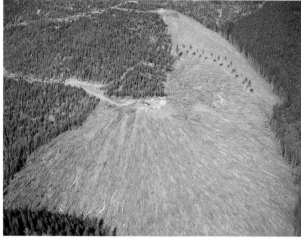

(Right) Clearcut softwood forest. Once the trees are removed, this area of Washington State will be replanted as part of a managed forest policy.

When a tree is felled, it is still surrounded by its bark. It can be removed before transportation or at the mill.

In the case of wood destined to be construction timber or furniture, care is taken to keep the log from damage by leaving on the bark. But that is an expensive way to transport logs. When the tree is destined to be used for pulp, chips, or chemicals, it is often better to process the entire tree in the forest, stripping off the branches and bark and chipping up the logs near where the tree was felled. The chips can then be put into a large container on a truck or in some circumstances even transported to the mill by special pipelines.

(Right) Round-wood trees drying in stacks before use.

Tree products

When trees are felled, their use is probably already known. It will be determined by the type of wood, the distance to market it has to be carried, the tallness and straightness of the trunks, and how much that kind of wood is worth in the marketplace.

Direct use

A small number of trees are used as natural poles and posts, for example, for holding up telephone and electricity wires, as supports in mines, as pilings under buildings in soft ground, or as supports for highway barriers. In the past they were also used for fortifications. Trees for this kind of use have to be fairly small in girth, straight, tall, and free from major defects. They are all intended for use outside in all weathers or to be sunk in permanently waterlogged ground and so must be pressure treated with preservatives to ensure they will not rot easily.

(Right) Whole trunk used as utility pole.

(Left and below) Pit props in mines and fence posts are two of the uses for round wood.

Rough sawing

LUMBER is the name given in the wood industry to wood that is sawn for use as whole pieces. Larger pieces of lumber—designed for use in building construction—are called TIMBER (although in general usage "timber" is a much more widely applied term).

Sawing takes place at the sawmill. The logs are stacked in the grounds of the mill, either floating in large ponds (if there is room) or in tall piles. Stacks of logs have to be constantly kept slightly moist with mists of water in summer; otherwise they will dry out, and the gases being released may become a fire hazard.

As each log is needed, it is brought into the mill and first taken through a debarking machine. This machine goes around and around the log, stripping the bark like an apple peeler.

The log is now ready for the headsaw—the first saw in the process. Usually it is a band saw, which is a thin metal ribbon with teeth that runs between pulleys. It makes a thin cut and so is less wasteful than the other main type of saw, the circular saw. If the wood is to be cut into known lengths, several saws may be combined on one frame. This is known as a gang saw.

The machine operator already knows what size of lumber or board to cut, and that will determine how to control the saw. Between cuttings the log is often turned so that it can be cut in more that one direction. The objective is to get as much useful wood from the log as possible.

Sawn planks are carried by conveyor and stacked and loaded onto trucks.

Sawdust and chippings can be used for paper and chipboard.

(Above) A sawmill requires a large amount of space both for its raw materials and its finished products.

Offices

Rough bark stripping and round timber grading

Saws are housed in this part of the mill.

Bark taken out of factory and used for mulch and fuel

Logs with bark brought in and stacked

(Above) A sawmill band saw.

(Above) Collecting logs from a stack before taking them to the sawmill.

(Below) Sawn timber stacked for drying.

Thus, for example, a headsaw may make the first cut. The log pieces are then turned, and a conveyor belt takes the turned-over log to a second saw that can then cut the log into boards.

The first sawings often produce thick boards. For that reason much of the sawn wood is resawn to make thinner boards, planks, and so on. However, at this stage it is not cut to sizes for selling except to wholesalers or those who will saw the wood again. That is because the wood is still damp and will change size as it dries. Only after drying will it be safe to cut it to final dimensions.

However, before some wood is dried, it is first steamed. This steaming process makes the wood darker. Such wood is chosen by the quality furniture industry.

Drying

All of the wood cut by the saws is still wet and is only rough-cut. Much of it still has irregular sides because it has not been trimmed. Before it can be sold for use, it has to be dried. It is not dried as logs because it would take a very long time for moisture to get out from the inside of a log. Instead, the wood is first cut into lumber as described above. That increases its surface area enormously and so makes it easier for the wood to dry.

Drying can take place in the open air, in kilns, or first in the air and then in a kiln. Air drying is preferred for high-quality timber, where further shrinkage or warping is to be avoided. The quality furniture industry, for example, prefers air-dried wood to kiln-dried wood.

In air drying, planks are stacked with blocks in between to separate them. The objective is to reduce the moisture down to about a fifth of the amount the wood had when it came into the mill. It will then be allowed to dry for even longer in the warehouse of the furniture maker. It takes up to a year for a 1-inch (2.5-cm) plank to dry. Drying can be made quicker by using fans.

Kiln drying is faster and cheaper since the land needed for storage is so much less. To kiln dry wood, it is stacked and blocked on a trolley and placed in a kiln,

which is a large oven. The source of the heat is steam circulating in pipes around the kiln walls.

The temperature and humidity of the air are controlled to make the wood dry as fast as possible. However, it cannot be done too quickly, otherwise the wood might split. Kilns are run at temperatures between 40 and 70°C. That is a good, but not too fast, drying temperature that will also kill insects.

Air is continually circulated using fans. It draws the moisture from the wood. The moist air is then blown out of the kiln.

Kiln drying of a 1-inch (2.5-cm) plank will taken moisture down from green to only 6% in a few days. However, kiln drying leaves stresses in the wood, and it may further change shape when it is exposed to the air again. That is why kiln-dried timber is not used for better-quality construction.

(Above and below) Rotary saws cutting dried planks into salable products. The machines make cuts into the planks, then turn the lumber and recut until pieces of the desired shape are obtained. The wood surface is then planed and sanded to reach its final size and produce a smooth surface.

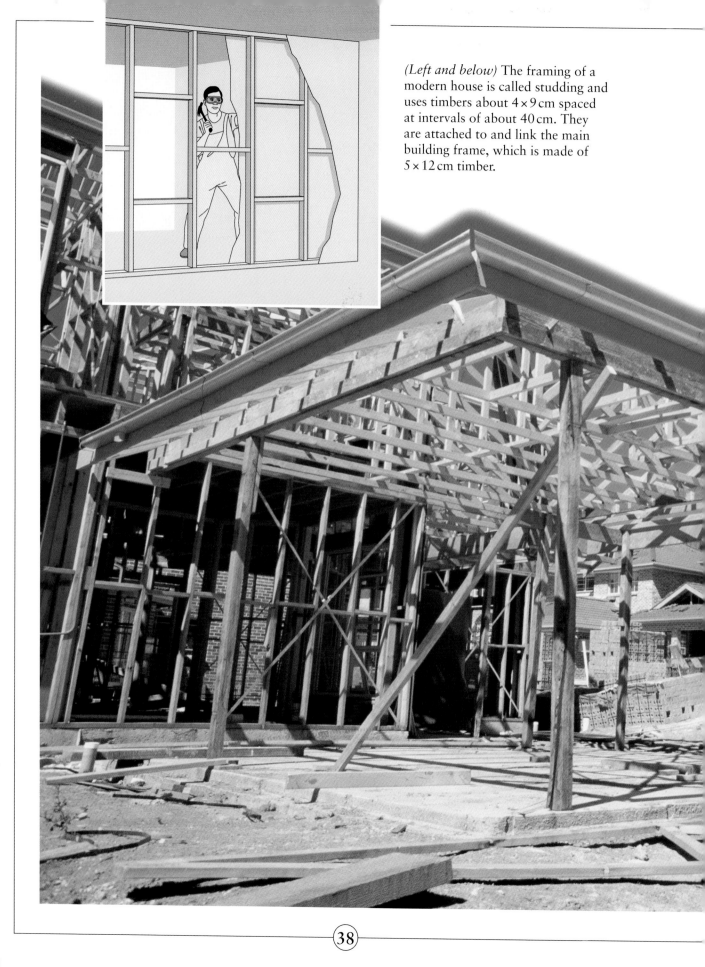

(*Left and below*) The framing of a modern house is called studding and uses timbers about 4 × 9 cm spaced at intervals of about 40 cm. They are attached to and link the main building frame, which is made of 5 × 12 cm timber.

Final cutting and turning

Once the timber has been roughly sawn up into planks and dried, the final cutting and shaping can be done with the confidence that the wood is now unlikely to change shape or size very much (unless it is allowed to get wet). This material is sold on to wholesale timber merchants or finds its way to retail outlets. It is also the material that is made into finely shaped wooden articles such as stair rails and bowls.

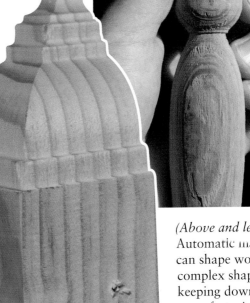

(Above and left) Automatic machines can shape wood into complex shapes, thus keeping down the manufacturing cost.

(Above) Demonstration of hand-turning skills at a craft fair. Most craftspeople prefer air-dried wood for its superior stability.

Preserving wood

Wood is a natural material. When it is cut down, it is seen as dead wood and therefore good food for a huge variety of plants, animals, and fungi. If wood is to be given a long life—especially outdoors—then it must be preserved in some way.

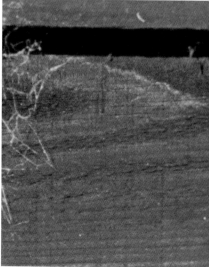

(Above) This untreated spade handle shows the reasons for using a preservative chemical —the handle has been fatally weakened by wood-boring beetles.

(Left) Pressure-treated wood used as fencing posts.

(Below) Creosote, a derivative of petroleum, is a traditional preservative.

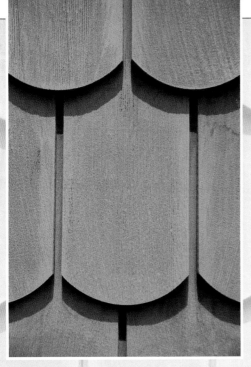

(Above and below) The color of this wood was produced by the preservative applied to it.

The simplest way of preserving timber against attack by fungus is to make sure the wood has a moisture content below 20%. That is normally easy to reach indoors, and it is why wood intended for indoor use is not treated with a preservative. Wood kept under water also does not decay because there is not enough oxygen for fungi to live. That is why ancient wooden remains have survived in peat bogs and estuary muds for thousands of years.

Wood is most likely to decay if it is placed in contact with moist soil, for the soil is a source of both water and fungi. Moisture contents in wood are higher in the open air than indoors even for wood used above ground, and so all exterior wood has to be treated to preserve it.

To make wood last in these conditions, it is treated with chemicals that kill fungi and often boring insects as well. There are many ways of doing this, from simple painting and spraying to immersion in a bath under pressure. Most commercial fence posts are sold with a label stating they have been treated with preservative under pressure. That is why modern posts last so much longer than old posts. Many of them have a slight green coloration as a result of the preservative treatment.

Processing wood for special products

The majority of the wood cut from logs is used as construction timber. However, there is also a significant demand for speciality products. They are known as ENGINEERED WOOD PRODUCTS and include veneer, plywood, glulam (glued laminated lumber), and oriented strand board.

Veneer

A veneer is a very thin sheet of wood (normally less than 0.8 of a millimeter). It is chosen for the decorative beauty of the wood. By taking very thin layers from a sheet of fine wood and sticking these veneers onto the surface of furniture made from ordinary wood, many pieces of furniture can have veneers. It is a much more economical way of using fine wood than making wood from solid high-cost lumber.

For high-quality veneers the wood is sliced, meaning it is cut sheet by sheet from a good log. This is the veneer used on expensive furniture. However, over 90% of veneers are destined for less glamorous locations, and they are rotary cut, much like using a potato peeler. These less-precise veneers make the outer layers of plywood.

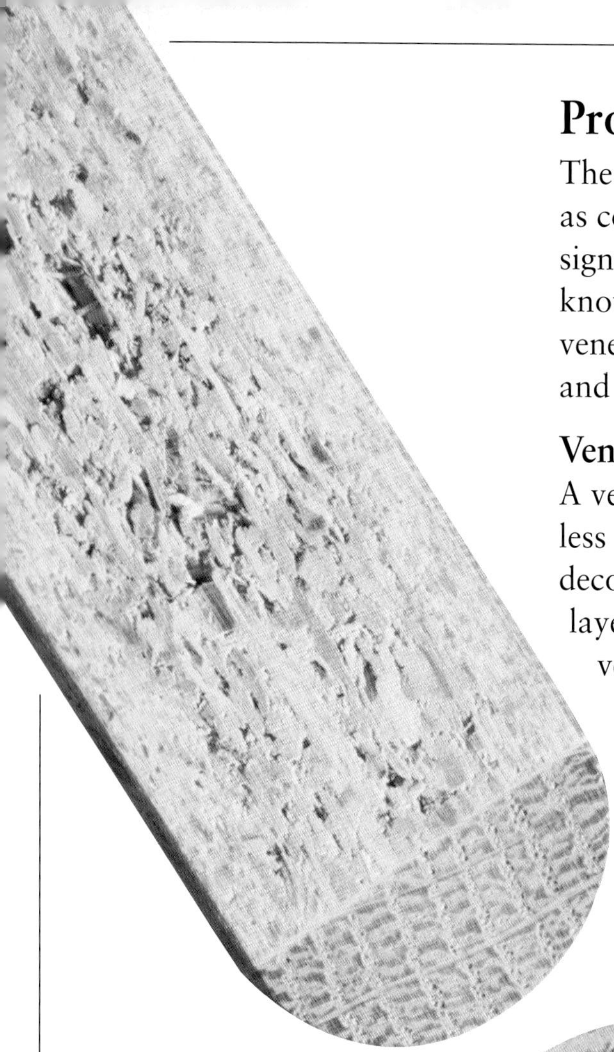

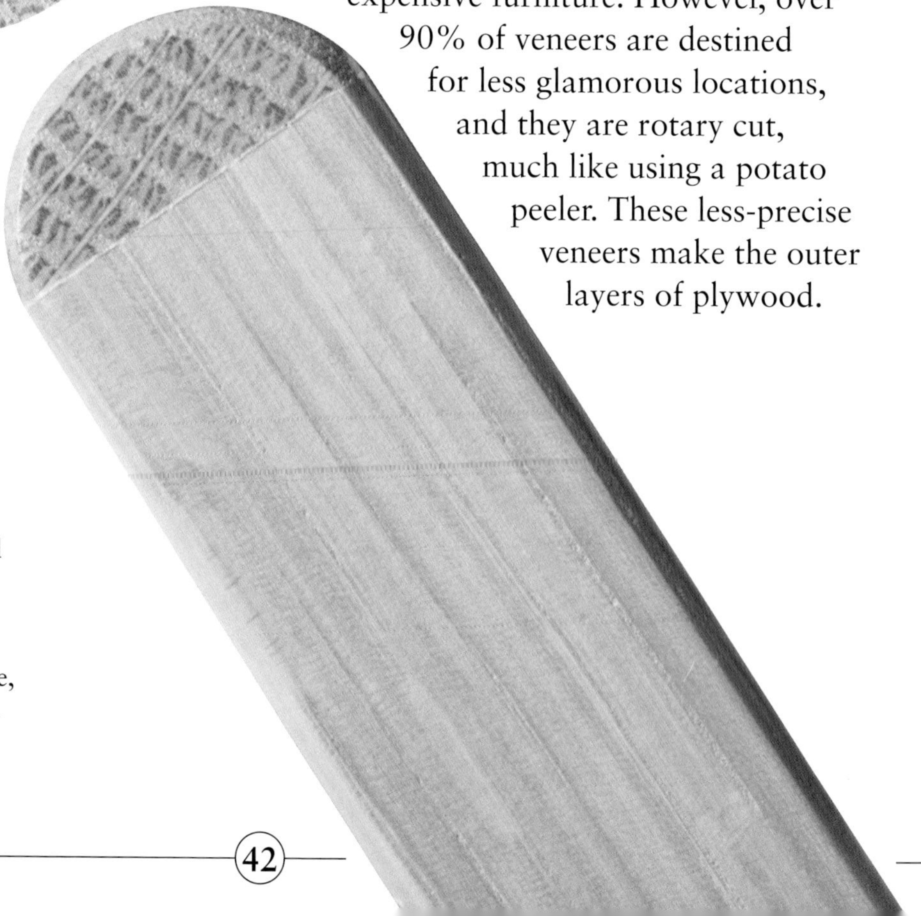

(Above and right) How veneers improve the surface of woods. The upper picture shows a bookcase shelf that has a real wood round-nosed edge applied only to the front. The rest is clearly chipboard. The picture on the right shows a shelf that has been veneered down the side, giving it the appearance of solid wood. The veneer is beech.

(Right and below) Furniture with wood veneers applied to the surface.

See **Vol. 6: Dyes, paints, and adhesives** *for more on plywood.*

(Above) Veneered plywood.

Plywood

Plywood is an example of a board made out of layers of wood that are glued together. Three or more layers, or plies, are used. The outer plies are veneers; the inner ply is solid wood or even re-formed chipwood. This inner layer does not use a sheet of solid wood but is made of offcuts of wood of the same thickness that are glued together. In this way a relatively cheap board can be made from inexpensive and often waste products.

Plywood does not warp easily because each layer is laid with its grain at right angles to the layer next to it. That provides balancing stresses in the plies.

Most plywood plies are stuck together with natural glues such as animal and starch glues, but synthetic resins such as urea-formaldehyde are also used. The synthetic adhesives are very resistant to attack by weather and decay. When they are used, the plywood is known as exterior grade or marine ply.

Plywood sheets can be shaped by heating them with steam and then putting them in a press. The adhesive is inserted at the same time, so the plies set in the desired curved shape. These kinds of curved plywoods are used to make the hulls of boats and some kinds of furniture.

Particleboard, chipboard, and oriented strand board

Another way of making laminated board is to grind the wood up into flakes, then reconstitute it by binding it with synthetic resin adhesives. This produces particleboard, chipboard, and oriented strand board. They are used, for example, as wall and roof sheeting in the building industry.

(Below and right) Larger buildings, such as this hotel, are often made with a steel and concrete frame and then sided in particleboard for insulation and strength before a brick or other finish is added to the outside. Oriented strand board is also an important material for absorbing earthquake waves in quake-prone areas.

(Left) Particles of wood mixed with resin make a hard, dense material that can be cut into precise shapes. This removes many of the problems associated with natural lumber such as warping and uneven response to stress.

Fiberboard

Fiberboard goes one step further than particleboard and uses the individual fibers of wood. In this case the wood fibers have to be separated by the chemical process of making pulp. Very low-quality wood can be used for this kind of board.

Once the fibers have been separated out as pulp, they can be shaped and then pressed, squeezing out much of the water. This is called felting. There are two kinds of such processing, known as wet felting and dry felting. Wet felting is a pressure process, and an adhesive is not used. In dry felting adhesive is used. Since the dry process produces less polluted water, it is more common.

The panel board produced is soft and easily damaged and so is best used in places where there is little wear. Some fiberboard has a paper surface glued onto it to make it more durable.

5: Paper

Wood is not just used in its original form. Very large amounts of it are also processed. The largest user of processed wood is the paper and board industry.

Almost all papers and boards such as cardboard are made from wood fibers. Paper is not used just for books and newspapers, but also in such varied areas as packaging, toweling, insulating, and construction.

How paper is made

Paper, whose name comes from papyrus, a reed originally used as a writing material in ancient Egypt, is a matted or FELTED sheet formed by trapping a suspension of fibers on a wire screen.

For many centuries paper was made one sheet at a time. A wire frame was pulled through the watery pulp and then lifted out. Once the surplus water had drained from the paper and it could be handled, it was lifted from the frame and put, together with many others, in a press, where it was made flat.

This was a very laborious method and gave little control over the paper thickness (called paper weight) or uniformity of the sheet. Then, in 1798 Nicolas-Louis Robert made a belt that moved and could take a continuous flow of pulp. From then on, it was possible to produce a long sheet of paper. Instead of being put onto a press, the wet paper was passed through rollers. This revolutionized the speed at which paper could be made.

Pressing the paper through the rollers removes most of the water, but it still needs to be dried. That is done with heaters. If required, the surface is then coated with materials that will give it a finer finish.

Most paper is made from cellulose fibers. They are not water resistant because they have no waxes or oils in them, and so they readily soak up water, swelling as they do so. That is why they soak

See **Vol. 7: Fibers** *for more on cardboard.*

(Below) Wood fibers still encrusted with lignin, gums, and resins.

(*Left and below*) Paper being handmade from sisal fibers. A suspension of the fibers in water is poured into a tray, which has a fine sieve in its base. The fibers are spread so that they settle in an even layer. The water is then drained off, leaving wet paper that can be decorated (here with flowers) and can receive another layer of fibers.

The cut paper is then dried on racks in the sun.

up moisture from the air—hence the common experience of paper becoming limp instead of staying crisp when it is in a moist environment.

But this property also has advantages. Wet cellulose fibers are as strong as dry ones, which makes it possible to handle paper and get it onto rollers while it is still wet.

Early paper fibers

The raw material of paper is a suspension of fibers. The first papers, made from papyrus, were produced by the time-consuming method of stripping the fibers from the stem of the plant, setting them out side by side in a layer, and then adding a further layer at right angles. This dry material was then wetted and pressed.

The papyrus plant sap contains a natural adhesive, and as it got wet, the adhesive seeped out of the fibers and stuck them together. The sheets were then allowed to dry. These early beginnings show the principles employed in papermaking up to the present day.

Papyrus paper was an important step in the development of modern paper, but it was not the only source of material that could easily be used. In China, for example, there was no papyrus, but there was lots of rice. So this plant was used instead. By A.D. 105 Ts'ai Lun in China had also used mulberry plants and many other fibers, including fishnets, old rags, and hemp waste, to make paper. Indeed, it seems that any naturally fibrous material could be made into paper.

Tree fibers

Interestingly, early papermaking did not make use of tree fiber. In part this was because of the difficulty of using wood fiber and in part because until the demand for paper for books grew, there was plenty of traditional material. But the printing press brought heavy additional demands.

Wood is more difficult to use because it consists of fibers intermixed with nonfibrous materials. The useful part of the wood for paper is the fibrous cellulose, but it is naturally encrusted in a hard, unwanted material called lignin.

Cellulose fibers (which are natural starch molecules that link end to end) are long and strong, and can be bent and twisted without breaking.

Two ways of separating the cellulose from the lignin were tried. One was entirely mechanical, grinding up the wood and making it into a pulp with water. But the pulp still contained lignin and could not be used to make white paper.

The other route used chemicals to dissolve the lignin and other unwanted materials, so that just the cellulose remained. This way is more expensive, but produces white paper of greater strength than groundwood paper.

Other sources of modern paper fibers

It is possible to make paper from any plant because all plants contain cellulose. However, the sheer volume of paper needed in the modern world means that just a few sources are tapped.

Wood is by far the most common modern raw material for paper. Just under half of all felled trees are used for making paper. The trunk of the tree is used because it contains the least amount of noncellulose material. Softwoods, such as conifers, are the preferred tree for papermaking because they have longer fibers—between 2 and 4 mm long. They also have a higher fiber content than hardwoods.

Nonwoody plants differ from wood in that they contain less cellulose and shorter fibers than wood. Papermaking with these plants, for example,

(Below) Various kinds of fibers can be used as a source for paper.

straw left over after cereal plants have been harvested, therefore produces more waste. If the nonfiber parts are not removed, the paper is stiff and tears easily.

One of the most successful nonwoody plant sources for paper is the residue from sugarcane processing (known as bagasse). It has a high fiber content, with long, fine fibers. It is a preferred choice in places where sugarcane is harvested but where trees are not abundant, as in some countries in South America.

Bamboo is another plant with a high fiber content. Its rapid growth makes it suitable as a large-scale, quickly replaced stock for paper making wherever it grows naturally, for example, in China. Flax is grown just for high-grade cigarette paper because it produces a very thin paper of high strength.

Rags provide cotton and linen fiber. These fibers produce greater strength and a finer finish than wood fibers. In part, that is because cotton and linen fibers are longer and finer than wood fibers. Rag fibers are still used for bank notes, where the paper is subjected to heavy handling but still has to last a long time. At the other end of the scale the very thin papers used, for example, in bibles need to be dense and durable. They, too, tend to be made from rags.

Rags are expensive to use because they have to be sorted by hand, and then they have to be boiled in giant pressure cookers to remove grease and other forms of dirt that they have acquired in their former use as clothing. The cleansing agents used for this process are lime (calcium hydroxide) and soda ash (sodium carbonate) or caustic soda (sodium hydroxide) and detergents.

The cooked fibers are beaten, which breaks them into shorter sections and frays out the fibers so they are flatter and cover more area. These fibers bond together exceptionally well, which accounts for their durability.

(Above and below) Bank notes have to be made of especially tough fibers in order to stand up to heavy wear.

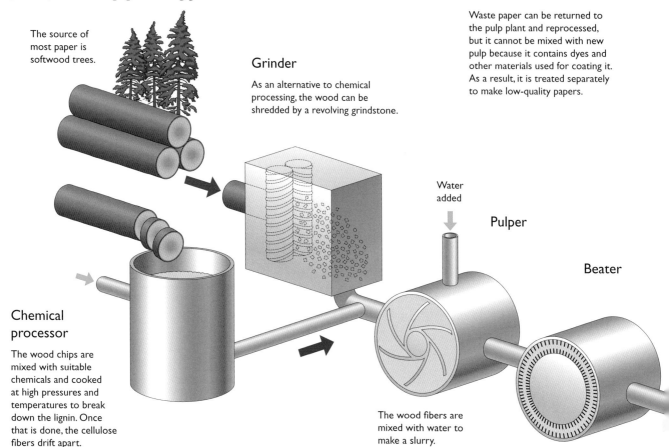

(Below) The basic papermaking process.

The source of most paper is softwood trees.

Grinder

As an alternative to chemical processing, the wood can be shredded by a revolving grindstone.

Waste paper can be returned to the pulp plant and reprocessed, but it cannot be mixed with new pulp because it contains dyes and other materials used for coating it. As a result, it is treated separately to make low-quality papers.

Water added

Pulper

Beater

Chemical processor

The wood chips are mixed with suitable chemicals and cooked at high pressures and temperatures to break down the lignin. Once that is done, the cellulose fibers drift apart.

The wood fibers are mixed with water to make a slurry.

The fibers can be further beaten to release natural adhesives.

The use of artificial fibers for paper

Artificial fibers can be made with any fiber shape and length desired, but their use has not been widespread due to the rising cost of the crude oil from which many are made. Rayon, the cheapest of the artificial fibers suited to papermaking, is several times more expensive than wood, and others are tens of times more costly. Artificials also have to be bonded together with an adhesive because they do not contain the natural adhesive that is found in cellulose. For specialized purposes, however, they come into their own. For example, in laboratories it is often necessary to filter solutions of acids. Filter papers made from natural fibers would be destroyed by acids, but synthetic fibers can be made that resist acids.

The stages of papermaking from wood

Pulp production

The first stage in papermaking is producing the pulp, which is a suspension of cellulose fibers in water. It is the raw material for the papermaking process.

The processing of paper is essentially a matter of chemistry. Chemicals work faster when there is a large surface area for them to act on, so the wood fiber is ground or crushed in a mill before being put into vats at high temperature and pressure. Here the lignin in the fiber is dissolved using either only sulfite salts or caustic soda (sodium hydroxide) and sodium sulfide. This latter set of chemicals is known as the kraft process ("kraft" is the German word for "strong")

Additives

Chemicals are added to the fibers to make the paper smooth, strong, and opaque. Sizing is added for water resistance. China clay adds gloss, and dyes can be used to add color.

Wet end

Stacks of calender rollers smooth the surface of the paper or can create surface effects.

Wire mesh belt

Drains paper

Wool felt belt

Soaks up much of the remaining moisture

The remaining water is removed by pressing the paper between rollers. A hot air drier can also be used at this stage.

Web of paper

Rolls of paper being taken for use by printers or packaging manufacturers.

Sheets of paper are wound onto rolls.

because it produces a stronger pulp than the sulfite process. It dominates the modern chemical pulp-making industry.

Once the lignin has been made soluble, the cellulose fibers drift apart and can be collected for the next stage of the papermaking process, often bleaching.

Many papers are not subject to complete lignin removal and bleaching because of the expense. As a result, they still contain some lignin, together with resins and other materials. When exposed to light, these materials turn yellow, which is why newspaper and some cheaper paperback books yellow within a matter of months, sometimes weeks.

Bleaching

Early papers were not particularly white. That is because natural cellulose is a pale cream color. But the discovery of chlorine in the late 18th century led to finding that it could be used as a bleaching agent to remove unwanted color and make paper whiter.

A variety of chemicals are used for bleaching. Traditionally, calcium and sodium hypochlorites were used. However, these chemicals will not work on pulp produced by the kraft process because it contains substances that stop hypochlorite from working. As a result, bleaching is done in a number of stages.

First, chlorine gas is mixed with the pulp. It does not bleach the pulp but combines with some of the ingredients in the pulp, which can then be washed away. The pulp goes through a dilute solution of caustic soda, and only after this is the pulp bleached with hypochlorite.

The result of bleaching can be substantial. The best bleached paper is half as bright again as unbleached paper.

(Below) Newspaper is not fully bleached and so quickly changes color. That is acceptable because newspapers have a life of only a single day.

20
TH
TOD
RAIN
SPR
Gen

Final pulp treatment

Pulp fibers need one final stage of treatment before they can be used for paper. The fibers are still mostly intact and so do not absorb water, nor do they give out the natural adhesive that enables them to stick together. In order to get the pulp fibers into a suitably frayed state, therefore, the pulp is often run through machines that fray the fibers. This process is called defibering. Modified versions of beating machines, called refiners, are used in continuous papermaking systems.

(Above) Photocopier paper does not need to prevent inks soaking in to its surface because the copying process presses carbon directly into the paper surface. A very highly coated surface would not be suitable, so the surface is relatively coarse.

See **Vol. 6: Dyes, paints, and adhesives** *for more on animal glue.*

Finishes

Whichever route is taken to make paper, the final product soaks up water. As a result, it cannot be used directly for printing because the inks will sink in and spread. To overcome this problem, the surface needs to be treated with a material that repels water. This is called SIZING. The substance used is essentially a very thin adhesive such as rosin.

Traditionally, size was made by boiling up animal bones or vegetables to release their adhesives. It was then diluted to an appropriate consistency that would soak into the paper yet leave the surface suitable for writing or printing. All of this was done sheet by sheet by hand. However, in 1800 Moritz Illing developed a method using rosin from trees, together with alum (aluminum sulfate), a material that helps chemicals stick to fibers (and is known as a mordant).

Paper is not just fiber. It consists of many other materials incorporated into the fiber to make better finishes. High-quality, smooth-surfaced paper, for example, uses kaolinite, or china clay, contained in an adhesive such as starch or a synthetic material such as LATEX. It is used as a filler between the fibers on all smooth-surfaced papers. It also makes the paper more opaque, so that thinner papers can be used and the printing on one side still not be visible on the other.

The amount of filler is usually just a few percent, but can be up to 10% by volume. China clay is cheaper than fiber, and so there is also a cost incentive to use it. China clay also adds to the weight of the paper, literally making it heavier. That makes paper feel of higher quality, since many people relate weight per sheet to quality in paper.

See **Vol. 4: Ceramics** *for more on china clay.*

See **Vol. 1: Plastics** *for more on latex.*

Strengthening agents

Papers can be strengthened by using various natural adhesives, such as starch, resins, and natural gums, such as locust bean gum. If papers need to be strong when wet, they need special adhesives, often resins, because natural fibers lose all their strength in water. Toilet tissue is one example where wet-strength is vital.

See **Vol. 6: Dyes, paints, and adhesives** *for more on pigments.*

Coloring

Papers can be colored by adding dyes or pigments to the finished pulp. PIGMENTS other than clay include titanium dioxide and calcium carbonate.

Papermaking

Once the pulp has been processed, it is called paper stock. It is fed into a machine that runs it over a moving wire screen to produce an even thickness of fibers. It is then pressed and rolled to remove excess water, dried, and then wound onto rolls. Such machines can produce paper at the rate of about a kilometer a minute.

Types of finished paper

Papers come in many kinds. Chief among them, however, are these:

Bond paper is used for high-quality writing paper. It often contains a large percentage of cotton fiber and is sometimes entirely made of cotton fiber.

Book paper is chemical woodpulp for good-quality books and mechanically ground pulp for inexpensive paperbacks. To make books appear bulkier and therefore better value, some are made with soda-treated pulp, which has a high bulk. For books containing photographs such as this one, coated papers have to be used. The coating can be china clay or titanium oxide pressed into the paper during papermaking.

(Below) Modern book printing is done on coated papers that prevent too much absorption of inks. Inks that dry on the surface of the paper are more vibrant than those that sink in.

(Below) Printing is done on large, fast machines, that dry as well as apply, the ink.

Newsprint papers are some of the poorest-quality papers made. They are mainly groundwood pulp. They are bulky and take ink well, but readily turn yellow when exposed to the light.

Wrapping paper is made of unbleached paper that has been sized to make it remain reasonably strong if it gets wet. Paper that is expected to get wet, such as that used for fresh foods, is often treated with resins.

Sanitary papers include toilet tissues and paper towels. They need to have a soft, bulky texture, and so they are hardly beaten during the pulp-making process. The softening is increased by a machine that presses the wet sheet against a smooth drying roll, then layers the sheets to create a multiply finish. This is called creping. All sanitary papers are given wet strength by using resins.

Most of the water in paper is actually held between the fibers. If a paper is to resist wetting, it has to be made less porous. Greaseproof paper, for example, is a low-porosity paper made by beating the pulp so hard that the fibers are very fine, and little space is left between them.

Recycling paper

Paper is made from fibers that are physically matted together. As a result, it is, in principle, a relatively simple task to unmat them and reuse the fibers in making new products. The reuse of paper reduces the need for more trees to be felled and puts less pressure on the remaining older forests. At the same time, it reduces the amount of waste paper that has to be put into landfill sites.

Recycling paper in practice is not that easy. That is because waste paper comes in many grades from cardboard and corrugated wrapping paper to printed newspapers. It is especially difficult to use recycled paper for high-quality paper because of the effort needed to get rid of the ink on the waste paper and provide a fine textured and high white finish. To remove the ink from recycled paper, the paper has to

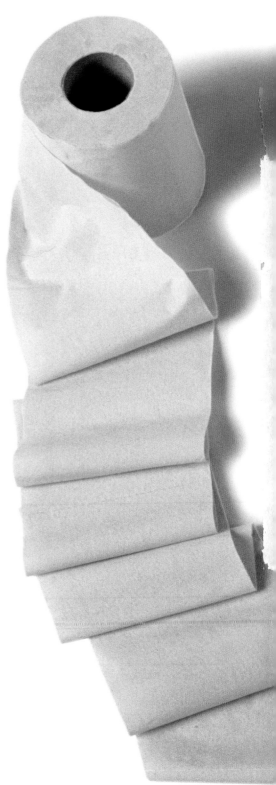

(Below) Toilet tissue needs to remain absorbent while wet.

(Below) Packaging material does not need to be of high quality, and so much of it uses recycled paper.

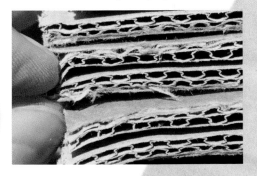

(Right) Paper does not have to be recycled into more paper. This paper has been ground up and is used for building insulation.

100% RECYCLED

(Above) There is a huge amount of waste paper produced. If it is not recycled, energy and natural resources are wasted.

be put in a vat of hot caustic soda (sodium hydroxide) and other chemicals such as detergents. The paper then has to be bleached with hypochlorite to whiten it. As a result, the vast majority of recycled paper is used without deinking for low-quality paper and especially for packaging materials.

Set Glossary

ACID RAIN: Rain that falls after having been contaminated by acid gases produced by power plants, vehicle exhausts, and other man-made sources.

ACIDITY: The tendency of a liquid to behave like an acid, reacting with metals and alkalis.

ADDITION POLYMERIZATION: The building blocks of many plastics (or polymers) are simple molecules called monomers. Monomers can be converted into polymers by making the monomers link to one another to form long chains in head-to-tail fashion. This is called addition polymerization or chain polymerization. It is most often used to link vinyl monomers to produce, for example, PVC, or polyvinyl chloride polymer.
See also **CONDENSATION POLYMERIZATION**

ADHESIVE: Any substance that can hold materials together simply by using some kind of surface attachment. In some cases this is a chemical reaction; in other cases it is a physical attraction between molecules of the adhesive and molecules of the substance it sticks to.

ADOBE: Simple unbaked brick made with mud, straw, and dung. It is dried in the open air. In this form it is very vulnerable to the effects of rainfall and so is most often found in desert areas or alternatively is protected by some waterproof covering, for example, thatch, straw, or reeds.

ALKALI: A base, or substance that can neutralize acids. In glassmaking an alkali is usually potassium carbonate and used as a flux to lower the melting point of the silica.

ALKYD: Any kind of synthetic resin used for protective coatings such as paint.

ALLOY: A metal mixture made up of two or more elements. Most of the elements used to make an alloy are metals. For example, brass is an alloy of copper and zinc, but carbon is an exception and used to make steel from iron.

AMALGAM: An alloy of mercury and one or more other metals. Dentist's filling amalgam traditionally contains mercury, silver, and tin.

AMPHIBIOUS: Adapted to function on both water and land.

AMORPHOUS: Shapeless and having no crystalline form. Glass is an amorphous solid.

ANION: An ion with a negative charge.

ANNEALING: A way of making a metal, alloy, or glass less brittle and more easy to work (more ductile) by heating it to a certain temperature (depending on the metal), holding it at that temperature for a certain time, and then cooling to room temperature.

ANODIZING: A method of plating metal by electrically depositing an oxide film onto the surface of a metal. The main purpose is to reduce corrosion.

ANTICYCLONE: A region of the Earth's atmosphere where the pressure is greater than average.

AQUEOUS SOLUTION: A substance dissolved in water.

ARTIFACT: An object of a previous time that was created by humans.

ARTIFICIAL DYE: A dye made from a chemical reaction that does not occur in nature. Dyes made from petroleum products are artificial dyes.

ARTIFICIAL FIBER: A fiber made from a material that has been manufactured, and that does not occur naturally. Rayon is an example of an artificial fiber.
Compare to **SYNTHETIC**

ATMOSPHERE: The envelope of gases that surrounds the Earth.

ATOM: The smallest particle of an element; a nucleus and its surrounding electrons.

AZO: A chemical compound that contains two nitrogen atoms joined by a double bond and each linked to a carbon atom. Azon compounds make up more than half of all dyes.

BARK: The exterior protective sheath of the stem and root of a woody plant such as a tree or a shrub. Everything beyond the cambium layer.

BAROMETER: An instrument for measuring atmospheric pressure.

BASE METAL: Having a low value and poorer properties than some other metals. Used, for example, when describing coins that contain metals other than gold or silver.

BAST FIBERS: A strong woody fiber that comes from the phloem of plants and is used for rope and similar products. Flax is an example of a bast fiber.

BATCH: A mixture of raw materials or products that are processes in a tank or kiln. This process produces small amounts of material or products and can be contrasted to continuous processes. Batch processing is used to make metals, alloys, glass, plastics, bricks, and other ceramics, dyes, and adhesives.

BAUXITE: A hydrated impure oxide of aluminum. It is the main ore used to obtain aluminum metal. The reddish-brown color of bauxite is caused by impurities of iron oxides.

BINDER: A substance used to make sure the pigment in a paint sticks to the surface it is applied to.

BIOCERAMICS: Ceramic materials that are used for medical and dental purposes, mainly as implants and replacements.

BLAST FURNACE: A tall furnace charged with a mixture of iron ore, coke, and limestone and used for the refining (smelting) of iron ore. The name comes from the strong blast of air used during smelting.

BLOWING: Forming a glass object by blowing into a gob of molten glass to form a bubble on the end of a blowpipe.

BOLL: The part of the cotton seed that contains the cotton fiber.

BOILING POINT: The temperature at which a liquid changes to a vapor. Boiling points change with atmospheric pressure.

BOND: A transfer or a sharing of electrons by two or more atoms. There are a number of kinds of chemical bonds, some very strong, such as covalent bonding and ionic bonding, and others quite weak, as in hydrogen bonding. Chemical bonds form because the linked molecules are more stable than the unlinked atoms from which they are formed.

BOYLE'S LAW: At constant temperature and for a given mass of gas the volume of the gas is inversely proportional to the pressure that builds up.

BRITTLE: Something that has almost no plasticity and so shatters rather than bends when a force is applied.

BULL'S EYE: A piece of glass with concentric rings marking the place where the blowpipe was attached to the glass. It is the central part of a pane of crown glass.

BUOYANCY: The tendency of an object to float if it is less dense than the liquid it is placed in.

BURN: A combustion reaction in which a flame is produced. A flame occurs where gases combust and release heat and light. At least two gases are therefore required if there is to be a flame.

CALORIFIC: Relating to the production of heat.

CAMBIUM: A thin growing layer that separates the xylem and phloem in most plants, and that produces new cell layers.

CAPACITOR: An electronic device designed for the temporary storage of electricity.

CAPILLARY ACTION, CAPILLARITY: The process by which surface tension forces can draw a liquid up a fine-bore tube.

CARBOHYDRATES: One of the main constituents of green plants, containing compounds of carbon, hydrogen, and oxygen. The main kinds of carbohydrate are sugars, starches, and celluloses.

CARBON COMPOUNDS: Any compound that includes the element carbon. Carbon compounds are also called organic compounds because they form an essential part of all living organisms.

CARBON CYCLE: The continuous movement of carbon between living things, the soil, the atmosphere, oceans, and rocks, especially those containing coal and petroleum.

CAST: To pour a liquid metal, glass, or other material into a mold and allow it to cool so that it solidifies and takes on the shape of the mold.

CATALYST: A substance that speeds up a chemical reaction but itself remains unchanged. For example, platinum is used in a catalytic converter of gases in the exhausts leaving motor vehicles.

CATALYTIC EFFECT: The way a substance helps speed up a reaction even though that substance does not form part of the reaction.

CATHODIC PROTECTION: The technique of protecting a metal object by connecting it to a more easily oxidizable material. The metal object being protected is made into the cathode of a cell. For example, iron can be protected by coupling it with magnesium.

CATION: An ion with a positive charge, often a metal.

CELL: A vessel containing two electrodes and a liquid substance that conducts electricity (an electrolyte).

CELLULOSE: A form of carbohydrate. *See* **CARBOHYDRATE**

CEMENT: A mixture of alumina, silica, lime, iron oxide, and magnesium oxide that is burned together in a kiln and then made into a powder. It is used as the main ingredient of mortar and as the adhesive in concrete.

CERAMIC: A crystalline nonmetal. In a more everyday sense it is a material based on clay that has been heated so that it has chemically hardened.

CHARRING: To burn partly so that some of a material turns to carbon and turns black.

CHINA: A shortened version of the original "Chinese porcelain," it also refers to various porcelain objects such as plates and vases meant for domestic use.

CHINA CLAY: The mineral kaolinite, which is a very white clay used as the basis of porcelain manufacture.

CLAY MINERALS: The minerals, such as kaolinite, illite, and montmorillonite, that occur naturally in soils and some rocks, and that are all minute platelike crystals.

COKE: A form of coal that has been roasted in the absence of air to remove much of the liquid and gas content.

COLORANTS: Any substance that adds a color to a material. The pigments in paints and the chemicals that make dyes are colorants.

COLORFAST: A dye that will not "run" in water or change color when it is exposed to sunlight.

COMPOSITE MATERIALS: Materials such as plywood that are normally regarded as a single material, but that themselves are made up of a number of different materials bonded together.

COMPOUND: A chemical consisting of two or more elements chemically bonded together, for example, calcium carbonate.

COMPRESSED AIR: Air that has been squashed to reduce its volume.

COMPRESSION: To be squashed.

COMPRESSION MOLDING: The shaping of an object, such as a headlight lens, which is achieved by squashing it into a mold.

CONCRETE: A mixture of cement and a coarse material such as sand and small stones.

CONDENSATION: The process of changing a gas to a liquid.

CONDENSATION POLYMERIZATION: The production of a polymer formed by a chain of reactions in which a water molecule is eliminated as every link of the polymer is formed. Polyester is an example.

CONDUCTION: (i) The exchange of heat (heat conduction) by contact with another object, or (ii) allowing the flow of electrons (electrical conduction).

CONDUCTIVITY: The property of allowing the flow of heat or electricity.

CONDUCTOR: (i) Heat—a material that allows heat to flow in and out of it easily. (ii) Electricity—a material that allows electrons to flow through it easily.

CONTACT ADHESIVE: An adhesive that, when placed on the surface to be joined, sticks as soon as the surfaces are placed firmly together.

CONVECTION: The circulating movement of molecules in a liquid or gas as a result of heating it from below.

CORRODE/CORROSION: A reaction usually between a metal and an acid or alkali in which the metal decomposes. The word is used in the sense of the metal being eaten away and dangerously thinned.

CORROSIVE: Causing corrosion, that is, the oxidation of a metal. For example, sodium hydroxide is corrosive.

COVALENT BONDING: The most common type of strong chemical bond, which occurs when two atoms share electrons. For example, oxygen O_2.

CRANKSHAFT: A rodlike piece of a machine designed to change linear into rotational motion or vice versa.

CRIMP: To cause to become wavy.

CRUCIBLE: A ceramic-lined container for holding molten metal, glass, and so on.

CRUDE OIL: A chemical mixture of petroleum liquids. Crude oil forms the raw material for an oil refinery.

CRYSTAL: A substance that has grown freely so that it can develop external faces.

CRYSTALLINE: A solid in which the atoms, ions, or molecules are organized into an orderly pattern without distinct crystal faces.

CURING: The process of allowing a chemical change to occur simply by waiting a while. Curing is often a process of reaction with water or with air.

CYLINDER GLASS: An old method of making window glass by blowing a large bubble of glass, then swinging it until it forms a cylinder. The ends of the cylinder are then cut off with shears and the sides of the cylinder allowed to open out until they form a flat sheet.

DECIDUOUS: A plant that sheds its leaves seasonally.

DECOMPOSE: To rot. Decomposing plant matter releases nutrients back to the soil and in this way provides nourishment for a new generation of living things.

DENSITY: The mass per unit volume (for example, g/c^3).

DESICCATE: To dry up thoroughly.

DETERGENT: A cleaning agent that is able to turn oils and dirts into an emulsion and then hold them in suspension so they can be washed away.

DIE: A tool for giving metal a required shape either by striking the object with the die or by forcing the object over or through the die.

DIFFUSION: The slow mixing of one substance with another until the two substances are evenly mixed. Mixing occurs because of differences in concentration within the mixture. Diffusion works rapidly with gases, very slowly with liquids.

DILUTE: To add more of a solvent to a solution.

DISSOCIATE: To break up. When a compound dissociates, its molecules break up into separate ions.

DISSOLVED: To break down a substance in a solution without causing a reaction.

DISTILLATION: The process of separating mixtures by condensing the vapors through cooling. The simplest form of distillation uses a Liebig condenser arranged with just a slight slope down to the collecting vessel. When the liquid mixture is heated and vapors are produced, they enter the water cooled condenser and then flow down the tube, where they can be collected.

DISTILLED WATER: Water that has its dissolved solids removed by the process of distillation.

DOPING: Adding an impurity to the surface of a substance in order to change its properties.

DORMANT: A period of inactivity such as during winter, when plants stop growing.

DRAWING: The process in which a piece of metal is pulled over a former or through dies.

DRY-CLEANED: A method of cleaning fabrics with nonwater-based organic solvents such as carbon tetrachloride.

DUCTILE: Capable of being drawn out or hammered thin.

DYE: A colored substance that will stick to another substance so that both appear to be colored.

EARLY WOOD: The wood growth put on the spring of each year.

EARTHENWARE: Pottery that has not been fired to the point where some of the clay crystals begin to melt and fuse together and is thus slightly porous and coarser than stoneware or porcelain.

ELASTIC: The ability of an object to regain its original shape after it has been deformed.

ELASTIC CHANGE: To change shape elastically.

ELASTICITY: The property of a substance that causes it to return to its original shape after it has been deformed in some way.

ELASTIC LIMIT: The largest force that a material can stand before it changes shape permanently.

ELECTRODE: A conductor that forms one terminal of a cell.

ELECTROLYSIS: An electrical-chemical process that uses an electric current to cause the breakup of a compound and the movement of metal ions in a solution. It is commonly used in industry for purifying (refining) metals or for plating metal objects with a fine, even metal coat.

ELECTROLYTE: An ionic solution that conducts electricity.

ELECTROMAGNET: A temporary magnet that is produced when a current of electricity passes through a coil of wire.

ELECTRON: A tiny, negatively charged particle that is part of an atom. The flow of electrons through a solid material such as a wire produces an electric current.

ELEMENT: A substance that cannot be decomposed into simpler substances by chemical means, for example, silver and copper.

EMULSION: Tiny droplets of one substance dispersed in another.

EMULSION PAINT: A paint made of an emulsion that is water soluble (also called latex paint).

ENAMEL: A substance made of finely powdered glass colored with a metallic oxide and suspended in oil so that it can be applied with a brush. The enamel is then heated, the oil burns away, and the glass fuses. Also used colloquially to refer to certain kinds of resin-based paint that have extremely durable properties.

ENGINEERED WOOD PRODUCTS: Wood products such as plywood sheeting made from a combination of wood sheets, chips or sawdust, and resin.

EVAPORATION: The change of state of a liquid to a gas. Evaporation happens below the boiling point.

EXOTHERMIC REACTION: A chemical reaction that gives out heat.

EXTRUSION: To push a substance through an opening so as to change its shape.

FABRIC: A material made by weaving threads into a network, often just referred to as cloth.

FELTED: Wool that has been hammered in the presence of heat and moisture to change its texture and mat the fibers.

FERRITE: A magnetic substance made of ferric oxide combined with manganese, nickel, or zinc oxide.

FIBER: A long thread.

FILAMENT: (i) The coiled wire used inside a light bulb. It consists of a high-resistance metal such as tungsten that also has a high melting point. (ii) A continuous thread produced during the manufacture of fibers.

FILLER: A material introduced in order to give bulk to a substance. Fillers are used in making paper and also in the manufacture of paints and some adhesives.

FILTRATE: The liquid that has passed through a filter.

FLOOD: When rivers spill over their banks and cover the surrounding land with water.

FLUID: Able to flow either as a liquid or a gas.

FLUORESCENT: A substance that gives out visible light when struck by invisible waves, such as ultraviolet rays.

FLUX: A substance that lowers the melting temperature of another substance. Fluxes are use in glassmaking and in melting alloys. A flux is used, for example, with a solder.

FORMER: An object used to control the shape or size of a product being made, for example, glass.

FOAM: A material that is sufficiently gelatinous to be able to contain bubbles of gas. The gas bulks up the substances, making it behave as though it were semirigid.

FORGE: To hammer a piece of heated metal until it changes to the desired shape.

FRACTION: A group of similar components of a mixture. In the petroleum industry the light fractions of crude oil are those with the smallest molecules, while the medium and heavy fractions have larger molecules.

FRACTIONAL DISTILLATION: The separation of the components of a liquid mixture by heating them to their boiling points.

FREEZING POINT: The temperature at which a substance undergoes a phase change from a liquid to a solid. It is the same temperature as the melting point.

FRIT: Partly fused materials of which glass is made.

FROTH SEPARATION: A process in which air bubbles are blown through a suspension, causing a froth of bubbles to collect on the surface. The materials that are attracted to the bubbles can then be removed with the froth.

FURNACE: An enclosed fire designed to produce a very high degree of heat for melting glass or metal or for reheating objects so they can be further processed.

FUSING: The process of melting particles of a material so they form a continuous sheet or solid object. Enamel is bonded to the surface of glass this way. Powder-formed metal is also fused into a solid piece. Powder paints are fused to the surface by heating.

GALVANIZING: The application of a surface coating of zinc to iron or steel.

GAS: A form of matter in which the molecules take no definite shape and are free to move around to uniformly fill any vessel they are put in. A gas can easily be compressed into a much smaller volume.

GIANT MOLECULES: Molecules that have been formed by polymerization.

GLASS: A homogeneous, often transparent material with a random noncrystalline molecular structure. It is achieved by cooling a molten substance very rapidly so that it cannot crystallize.

GLASS CERAMIC: A ceramic that is not entirely crystalline.

GLASSY STATE: A solid in which the molecules are arranged randomly rather than being formed into crystals.

GLOBAL WARMING: The progressive increase in the average temperature of the Earth's atmosphere, most probably in large part due to burning fossil fuels.

GLUE: An adhesive made from boiled animal bones.

GOB: A piece of near-molten glass used by glass-blowers and in machines to make hollow glass vessels.

GRAIN: (i) The distinctive pattern of fibers in wood. (ii) Small particles of a solid, including a single crystal.

GRAPHITE: A form of the element carbon with a sheetlike structure.

GRAVITY: The attractive force produced because of the mass of an object.

GREENHOUSE EFFECT: An increase in the global air temperature as a result of heat released from burning fossil fuels being absorbed by carbon dioxide in the atmosphere.

GREENHOUSE GAS: Any of various gases that contribute to the greenhouse effect, such as carbon dioxide.

GROUNDWATER: Water that flows naturally through rocks as part of the water cycle.

GUM: Any natural adhesive of plant origin that consists of colloidal polysaccharide substances that are gelatinous when moist but harden on drying.

HARDWOOD: The wood from a nonconiferous tree.

HEARTWOOD: The old, hard, nonliving central wood of trees.

HEAT: The energy that is transferred when a substance is at a different temperature than that of its surroundings.

HEAT CAPACITY: The ratio of the heat supplied to a substance compared with the rise in temperature that is produced.

HOLOGRAM: A three-dimensional image reproduced from a split laser beam.

HYDRATION: The process of absorption of water by a substance. In some cases hydration makes a substance change color, but in all cases there is a change in volume.

HYDROCARBON: A compound in which only hydrogen and carbon atoms are present. Most fuels are hydrocarbons, for example, methane.

HYDROFLUORIC ACID: An extremely corrosive acid that attacks silicate minerals such as glass. It is used to etch decoration onto glass and also to produce some forms of polished surface.

HYDROGEN BOND: A type of attractive force that holds one molecule to another. It is one of the weaker forms of intermolecular attractive force.

HYDROLYSIS: A reversible process of decomposition of a substance in water.

HYDROPHILIC: Attracted to water.

HYDROPHOBIC: Repelled by water.

IMMISCIBLE: Will not mix with another substance, for example, oil and water.

IMPURITIES: Any substances that are found in small quantities, and that are not meant to be in the solution or mixture.

INCANDESCENT: Glowing with heat, for example, a tungsten filament in a light bulb.

INDUSTRIAL REVOLUTION: The time, which began in the 18th century and continued through into the 19th century, when materials began to be made with the use of power machines and mass production.

INERT: A material that does not react chemically.

INORGANIC: A substance that does not contain the element carbon (and usually hydrogen), for example, sodium chloride.

INSOLUBLE: A substance that will not dissolve, for example, gold in water.

INSULATOR: A material that does not conduct electricity.

ION: An atom or group of atoms that has gained or lost one or more electrons and so developed an electrical charge.

IONIC BONDING: The form of bonding that occurs between two ions when the ions have opposite charges, for example, sodium ions bond with chloride ions to make sodium chloride. Ionic bonds are strong except in the presence of a solvent.

IONIZE: To change into ions.

ISOTOPE: An atom that has the same number of protons in its nucleus, but that has a different mass, for example, carbon 12 and carbon 14.

KAOLINITE: A form of clay mineral found concentrated as china clay. It is the result of the decomposition of the mineral feldspar.

KILN: An oven used to heat materials. Kilns at quite low temperatures are used to dry wood and at higher temperatures to bake bricks and to fuse enamel onto the surfaces of other substances. They are a form of furnace.

KINETIC ENERGY: The energy due to movement. When a ball is thrown, it has kinetic energy.

KNOT: The changed pattern in rings in wood due to the former presence of a branch.

LAMINATE: An engineered wood product consisting of several wood layers bonded by a resin. Also applies to strips of paper stuck together with resins to make such things as "formica" worktops.

LATE WOOD: Wood produced during the summer part of the growing season.

LATENT HEAT: The amount of heat that is absorbed or released during the process of changing state between gas, liquid, or solid. For example, heat is absorbed when liquid changes to gas. Heat is given out again as the gas condenses back to a liquid.

LATEX: A general term for a colloidal suspension of rubber-type material in water. Originally for the milky white liquid emulsion found in the Para rubber tree, but also now any manufactured water emulsion containing synthetic rubber or plastic.

LATEX PAINT: A water emulsion of a synthetic rubber or plastic used as paint. *See* **EMULSION PAINT**

LATHE: A tool consisting of a rotating spindle and cutters that is designed to produce shaped objects that are symmetrical about the axis of rotation.

LATTICE: A regular geometric arrangement of objects in space.

LEHR: The oven used for annealing glassware. It is usually a very long tunnel through which glass passes on a conveyor belt.

LIGHTFAST: A colorant that does not fade when exposed to sunlight.

LIGNIN: A form of hard cellulose that forms the walls of cells.

LIQUID: A form of matter that has a fixed volume but no fixed shape.

LUMBER: Timber that has been dressed for use in building or carpentry and consists of planed planks.

MALLEABLE: Capable of being hammered or rolled into a new shape without fracturing due to brittleness.

MANOMETER: A device for measuring liquid or gas pressure.

MASS: The amount of matter in an object. In common use the word weight is used instead (incorrectly) to mean mass.

MATERIAL: Anything made of matter.

MATTED: Another word for felted. *See* **FELTED**

MATTER: Anything that has mass and takes up space.

MELT: The liquid glass produced when a batch of raw materials melts. Also used to describe molten metal.

MELTING POINT: The temperature at which a substance changes state from a solid phase to a liquid phase. It is the same as the freezing point.

METAL: A class of elements that is a good conductor of electricity and heat, has a metallic luster, is malleable and ductile, and is formed as cations held together by a sea of electrons. A metal may also be an alloy of these elements and carbon.

METAL FATIGUE: The gradual weakening of a metal by constant bending until a crack develops.

MINERAL: A solid substance made of just one element or compound, for example, calcite minerals contain only calcium carbonate.

MISCIBLE: Capable of being mixed.

MIXTURE: A material that can be separated into two or more substances using physical means, for example, air.

MOLD: A containing shape made of wood, metal, or sand into which molten glass or metal is poured. In metalworking it produces a casting. In glassmaking the glass is often blown rather than poured when making, for example, light bulbs.

MOLECULE: A group of two or more atoms held together by chemical bonds.

MONOMER: A small molecule and building block for larger chain molecules or polymers (mono means "one" and mer means "part").

MORDANT: A chemical that is attracted to a dye and also to the surface that is to be dyed.

MOSAIC: A decorated surface made from a large number of small colored pieces of glass, natural stone, or ceramic that are cemented together.

NATIVE METAL: A pure form of a metal not combined as a compound. Native metals are more common in nonreactive elements such as gold than reactive ones such as calcium.

NATURAL DYES: Dyes made from plants without any chemical alteration, for example, indigo.

NATURAL FIBERS: Fibers obtained from plants or animals, for example, flax and wool.

NEUTRON: A particle inside the nucleus of an atom that is neutral and has no charge.

NOBLE GASES: The members of group 8 of the periodic table of the elements: helium, neon, argon, krypton, xenon, radon. These gases are almost entirely unreactive.

NONMETAL: A brittle substance that does not conduct electricity, for example, sulfur or nitrogen.

OIL-BASED PAINTS: Paints that are not based on water as a vehicle. Traditional artists' oil paint uses linseed oil as a vehicle.

OPAQUE: A substance through which light cannot pass.

ORE: A rock containing enough of a useful substance to make mining it worthwhile, for example, bauxite, the ore of aluminum.

ORGANIC: A substance that contains carbon and usually hydrogen. The carbonates are usually excluded.

OXIDE: A compound that includes oxygen and one other element, for example, Cu_2O, copper oxide.

OXIDIZE, OXIDIZING AGENT: A reaction that occurs when a substance combines with oxygen or a reaction in which an atom, ion, or molecule loses electrons to another substance (and in this more general case does not have to take up oxygen).

OZONE: A form of oxygen whose molecules contain three atoms of oxygen. Ozone high in the atmosphere blocks harmful ultraviolet rays from the Sun, but at ground level it is an irritant gas when breathed in and so is regarded as a form of pollution. The ozone layer is the uppermost part of the stratosphere.

PAINT: A coating that has both decorative and protective properties, and that consists of a pigment suspended in a vehicle, or binder, made of a resin dissolved in a solvent. It dries to give a tough film.

PARTIAL PRESSURE: The pressure a gas in a mixture would exert if it alone occupied the flask. For example, oxygen makes up about a fifth of the atmosphere. Its partial pressure is therefore about a fifth of normal atmospheric pressure.

PASTE: A thick suspension of a solid in a liquid.

PATINA: A surface coating that develops on metals and protects them from further corrosion, for example, the green coating of copper carbonate that forms on copper statues.

PERIODIC TABLE: A chart organizing elements by atomic number and chemical properties into groups and periods.

PERMANENT HARDNESS: Hardness in the water that cannot be removed by boiling.

PETROCHEMICAL: Any of a large group of manufactured chemicals (not fuels) that come from petroleum and natural gas. It is usually taken to include similar products that can be made from coal and plants.

PETROLEUM: A natural mixture of a range of gases, liquids, and solids derived from the decomposed remains of animals and plants.

PHASE: A particular state of matter. A substance can exist as a solid, liquid, or gas and may change between these phases with the addition or removal of energy, usually in the form of heat.

PHOSPHOR: A material that glows when energized by ultraviolet or electron beams, such as in fluorescent tubes and cathode ray tubes.

PHOTOCHEMICAL SMOG: A mixture of tiny particles of dust and soot combined with a brown haze caused by the reaction of colorless nitric oxide from vehicle exhausts and oxygen of the air to form brown nitrogen dioxide.

PHOTOCHROMIC GLASSES: Glasses designed to change color with the intensity of light. They use the property that certain substances, for example, silver halide, can change color (and change chemically) in light. For example, when silver chromide is dispersed in the glass melt, sunlight decomposes the silver halide to release silver (and so darken the lens). But the halogen cannot escape; and when the light is removed, the halogen recombines with the silver to turn back to colorless silver halide.

PHOTOSYNTHESIS: The natural process that happens in green plants whereby the energy from light is used to help turn gases, water, and minerals into tissue and energy.

PIEZOELECTRICS: Materials that produce electric currents when they are deformed, or vice versa.

PIGMENT: Insoluble particles of coloring material.

PITH: The central strand of spongy tissue found in the stems of most plants.

PLASTIC: Material—a carbon-based substance consisting of long chains or networks (polymers) of simple molecules. The word plastic is commonly used only for synthetic polymers. Property—a material is plastic if it can be made to change shape easily and then remain in this new shape (contrast with elasticity and brittleness).

PLASTIC CHANGE: A permanent change in shape that happens without breaking.

PLASTICIZER: A chemical added to rubbers and resins to make it easier for them to be deformed and molded. Plasticizers are also added to cement to make it more easily worked when used as a mortar.

PLATE GLASS: Rolled, ground, and polished sheet glass.

PLIABLE: Supple enough to be repeatedly bent without fracturing.

PLYWOOD: An engineered wood laminate consisting of sheets of wood bonded with resin. Each sheet of wood has the grain at right angles to the one above and below. This imparts stability to the product.

PNEUMATIC DEVICE: Any device that works with air pressure.

POLAR: Something that has a partial electric charge.

POLYAMIDES: A compound that contains more than one amide group, for example, nylon.

POLYMER: A compound that is made of long chains or branching networks by combining molecules called monomers as repeating units. Poly means "many," mer means "part."

PORCELAIN: A hard, fine-grained, and translucent white ceramic that is made of china clay and is fired to a high temperature. Varieties include china.

PORES: Spaces between particles that are small enough to hold water by capillary action, but large enough to allow water to enter.

POROUS: A material that has small cavities in it, known as pores. These pores may or may not be joined. As a result, porous materials may or may not allow a liquid or gas to pass through them. Popularly, porous is used to mean permeable, the kind of porosity in which the pores are joined, and liquids or gases can flow.

POROUS CERAMICS: Ceramics that have not been fired at temperatures high enough to cause the clays to fuse and so prevent the slow movement of water.

POTENTIAL ENERGY: Energy due to the position of an object. Water in a reservoir has potential energy because it is stored up, and when released, it moves down to a lower level.

POWDER COATING: The application of a pigment in powder form without the use of a solvent.

POWDER FORMING: A process of using a powder to fill a mold and then heating the powder to make it fuse into a solid.

PRECIPITATE: A solid substance formed as a result of a chemical reaction between two liquids or gases.

PRESSURE: The force per unit area measured in SI units in Pascals and also more generally in atmospheres.

PRIMARY COLORS: A set of colors from which all others can be made. In transmitted light they are red, blue, and green.

PROTEIN: Substances in plants and animals that include nitrogen.

PROTON: A positively charged particle in the nucleus of an atom that balances out the charge of the surrounding electrons.

QUENCH: To put into water in order to cool rapidly.

RADIATION: The transmission of energy from one body to another without any contribution from the intervening space. *Contrast with* **CONVECTION** and **CONDUCTION**

RADIOACTIVE: A substance that spontaneously emits energetic particles.

RARE EARTHS: Any of a group of metal oxides that are found widely throughout the Earth's rocks, but in low concentrations. They are mainly made up of the elements of the lanthanide series of the periodic table of the elements.

RAW MATERIAL: A substance that has not been prepared, but that has an intended use in manufacturing.

RAY: Narrow beam of light.

RAYON: An artificial fiber made from natural cellulose.

REACTION (CHEMICAL): The recombination of two substances using parts of each substance.

REACTIVE: A substance that easily reacts with many other substances.

RECYCLE: To take once used materials and make them available for reuse.

REDUCTION, REDUCING AGENT: The removal of oxygen from or the addition of hydrogen to a compound.

REFINING: Separating a mixture into the simpler substances of which it is made, especially petrochemical refining.

REFRACTION: The bending of a ray of light as it passes between substances of different refractive index (light-bending properties).

REFRACTORY: Relating to the use of a ceramic material, especially a brick, in high-temperature conditions of, for example, a furnace.

REFRIGERANT: A substance that, on changing between a liquid and a gas, can absorb large amounts of (latent) heat from its surroundings.

REGENERATED FIBERS: Fibers that have been dissolved in a solution and then recovered from the solution in a different form.

REINFORCED FIBER: A fiber that is mixed with a resin, for example, glass-reinforced fiber.

RESIN: A semisolid natural material that is made of plant secretions and often yellow-brown in color. Also synthetic materials with the same type of properties. Synthetic resins have taken over almost completely from natural resins and are available as thermoplastic resins and thermosetting resins.

RESPIRATION: The process of taking in oxygen and releasing carbon dioxide in animals and the reverse in plants.

RIVET: A small rod of metal that is inserted into two holes in metal sheets and then burred over at both ends in order to stick the sheets together.

ROCK: A naturally hard inorganic material composed of mineral particles or crystals.

ROLLING: The process in which metal is rolled into plates and bars.

ROSIN: A brittle form of resin used in varnishes.

RUST: The product of the corrosion of iron and steel in the presence of air and water.

SALT: Generally thought of as sodium chloride, common salt; however, more generally a salt is a compound involving a metal. There are therefore many "salts" in water in addition to sodium chloride.

SAPWOOD: The outer, living layers of the tree, which includes cells for the transportation of water and minerals between roots and leaves.

SATURATED: A state in which a liquid can hold no more of a substance dissolved in it.

SEALANTS: A material designed to stop water or other liquids from penetrating into a surface or between surfaces. Most sealants are adhesives.

SEMICONDUCTOR: A crystalline solid that has an electrical conductivity part way between a conductor and an insulator. This material can be altered by doping to control an electric current. Semiconductors are the basis of transistors, integrated circuits, and other modern electronic solid-state devices.

SEMIPERMEABLE MEMBRANE: A thin material that acts as a fine sieve or filter, allowing small molecules to pass, but holding back large molecules.

SEPARATING COLUMN: A tall glass tube containing a porous disk near the base and filled with a substance such as aluminum oxide that can absorb materials on its surface. When a mixture passes through the columns, fractions are retarded by differing amounts so that each fraction is washed through the column in sequence.

SEPARATING FUNNEL: A pear-shaped glass funnel designed to permit the separation of immiscible liquids by simply pouring off the more dense liquid from the bottom of the funnel, while leaving the less dense liquid in the funnel.

SHAKES: A defect in wood produced by the wood tissue separating, usually parallel to the rings.

SHEEN: A lustrous, shiny surface on a yarn. It is produced by the finishing process or may be a natural part of the yarn.

SHEET-METAL FORMING: The process of rolling out metal into sheet.

SILICA: Silicon dioxide, most commonly in the form of sand.

SILICA GLASS: Glass made exclusively of silica.

SINTER: The process of heating that makes grains of a ceramic or metal a solid mass before it becomes molten.

SIZE: A glue, varnish, resin, or similar very dilute adhesive sealant used to block up the pores in porous surfaces or, for example, plaster and paper. Once the size has dried, paint or other surface coatings can be applied without the coating sinking in.

SLAG: A mixture of substances that are waste products of a furnace. Most slag are mainly composed of silicates.

SMELTING: Roasting a substance in order to extract the metal contained in it.

SODA: A flux for glassmaking consisting of sodium carbonate.

SOFTWOOD: Wood obtained from a coniferous tree.

SOLID: A rigid form of matter that maintains its shape regardless of whether or not it is in a container.

SOLIDIFICATION: Changing from a liquid to a solid.

SOLUBILITY: The maximum amount of a substance that can be contained in a solvent.

SOLUBLE: Readily dissolvable in a solvent.

SOLUTION: A mixture of a liquid (the solvent) and at least one other substance of lesser abundance (the solute). Like all mixtures, solutions can be separated by physical means.

SOLVAY PROCESS: Modern method of manufacturing the industrial alkali sodium carbonate (soda ash).

SOLVENT: The main substance in a solution.

SPECTRUM: A progressive series arranged in order, for example, the range of colors that make up visible light as seen in a rainbow.

SPINNERET: A small metal nozzle perforated with many small holes through which a filament solution is forced. The filaments that emerge are solidified by cooling and the filaments twisted together to form a yarn.

SPINNING: The process of drawing out and twisting short fibers, for example, wool, and thus making a thread or yarn.

SPRING: A natural flow of water from the ground.

STABILIZER: A chemical that, when added to other chemicals, prevents further reactions. For example, in soda lime glass the lime acts as a stabilizer for the silica.

STAPLE: A short fiber that has to be twisted with other fibers (spun) in order to make a long thread or yarn.

STARCHES: One form of carbohydrate. Starches can be used to make adhesives.

STATE OF MATTER: The physical form of matter. There are three states of matter: liquid, solid, and gas.

STEAM: Water vapor at the boiling point of water.

STONEWARE: Nonwhite pottery that has been fired at a high temperature until some of the clay has fused, a state called vitrified. Vitrification makes the pottery impervious to water. It is used for general tableware, often for breakfast crockery.

STRAND: When a number of yarns are twisted together, they make a strand. Strands twisted together make a rope.

SUBSTANCE: A type of material including mixtures.

SULFIDE: A compound that is composed only of metal and sulfur atoms, for example, PbS, the mineral galena.

SUPERCONDUCTORS: Materials that will conduct electricity with virtually no resistance if they are cooled to temperatures close to absolute zero $(-273°C)$.

SURFACE TENSION: The force that operates on the surface of a liquid, and that makes it act as though it were covered with an invisible elastic film.

SURFACTANT: A substance that acts on a surface, such as a detergent.

SUSPENDED, SUSPENSION: Tiny particles in a liquid or a gas that do not settle out within time.

SYNTHETIC: Something that does not occur naturally but has to be manufactured. Synthetics are often produced from materials that do not occur in nature, for example, from petrochemicals. (i) Dye—a synthetic dye is made from petrochemicals, as opposed to natural dyes that are made of extracts of plants. (ii) Fiber—synthetic is a subdivision of artificial. Although both polyester and rayon are artificial fibers, rayon is made from reconstituted natural cellulose fibers and so is not synthetic, while polyester is made from petrochemicals and so is a synthetic fiber.

TANNIN: A group of pale-yellow or light-brown substances derived from plants that are used in dyeing fabric and making ink. Tannins are soluble in water and produce dark-blue or dark-green solutions when added to iron compounds.

TARNISH: A coating that develops as a result of the reaction between a metal and the substances in the air. The most common form of tarnishing is a very thin transparent oxide coating, such as occurs on aluminum. Sulfur compounds in the air make silver tarnish black.

TEMPER: To moderate or to make stronger: used in the metal industry to describe softening hardened steel or cast iron by reheating at a lower temperature or to describe hardening steel by reheating and cooling in oil; or in the glass industry, to describe toughening glass by first heating it and then slowly cooling it.

TEMPORARILY HARD WATER: Hard water that contains dissolved substances that can be removed by boiling.

TENSILE (PULLING STRENGTH): The greatest lengthwise (pulling) stress a substance can bear without tearing apart.

TENSION: A state of being pulled. Compare to compression.

TERRA COTTA: Red earth-colored glazed or unglazed fired clay whose origins lie in the Mediterranean region of Europe.

THERMOPLASTIC: A plastic that will soften and can be molded repeatedly into different shapes. It will then set into the molded shape as it cools.

THERMOSET: A plastic that will set into a molded shape as it first cools, but that cannot be made soft again by reheating.

THREAD: A long length of filament, group of filaments twisted together, or a long length of short fibers that have been spun and twisted together into a continuous strand.

TIMBER: A general term for wood suitable for building or for carpentry and consisting of roughcut planks. *Compare to* **LUMBER**

TRANSITION METALS: Any of the group of metallic elements (for example, chromium and iron) that belong to the central part of the periodic table of the elements and whose oxides commonly occur in a variety of colors.

TRANSPARENT: Something that will readily let light through, for example, window glass. Compare to translucent, when only some light gets through but an image cannot be seen, for example, greaseproof paper.

TROPOSPHERE: The lower part of the atmosphere in which clouds form. In general, temperature decreases with height.

TRUNK: The main stem of a tree.

VACUUM: Something from which all air has been removed.

VAPOR: The gaseous phase of a substance that is a liquid or a solid at that temperature, for example, water vapor is the gaseous form of water.

VAPORIZE: To change from a liquid to a gas, or vapor.

VENEER: A thin sheet of highly decorative wood that is applied to cheap wood or engineered wood products to improve their appearance and value.

VINYL: Often used as a general name for plastic. Strictly, vinyls are polymers derived from ethylene by removal of one hydrogen atom, for example, PVC, polyvinylchloride.

VISCOSE: A yellow-brown solution made by treating cellulose with alkali solution and carbon disulfide and used to make rayon.

VISCOUS, VISCOSITY: Sticky. Viscosity is a measure of the resistance of a liquid to flow. The higher the viscosity—the more viscous it is—the less easily it will flow.

VITREOUS CHINA: A translucent form of china or porcelain.

VITRIFICATION: To heat until a substance changes into a glassy form and fuses together.

VOLATILE: Readily forms a gas. Some parts of a liquid mixture are often volatile, as is the case for crude oil. This allows them to be separated by distillation.

WATER CYCLE: The continual interchange of water between the oceans, the air, clouds, rain, rivers, ice sheets, soil, and rocks.

WATER VAPOR: The gaseous form of water.

WAVELENGTH: The distance between adjacent crests on a wave. Shorter wavelengths have smaller distances between crests than longer wavelengths.

WAX: Substances of animal, plant, mineral, or synthetic origin that are similar to fats but are less greasy and harder. They form hard films that can be polished.

WEAVING: A way of making a fabric by passing two sets of yarns through one another at right angles to make a kind of tight meshed net with no spaces between the yarns.

WELDING: Technique used for joining metal pieces through intense localized heat. Welding often involves the use of a joining metal such as a rod of steel used to attach steel pieces (arc welding).

WETTING: In adhesive spreading, a term that refers to the complete coverage of an adhesive over a surface.

WETTING AGENT: A substance that is able to cover a surface completely with a film of liquid. It is a substance with a very low surface tension.

WHITE GLASS: Also known as milk glass, it is an opaque white glass that was originally made in Venice and meant to look like porcelain.

WROUGHT IRON: A form of iron that is relatively soft and can be bent without breaking. It contains less than 0.1% carbon.

YARN: A strand of fibers twisted together and used to make textiles.

Set Index

A

abrasive **4:** 6, 12
ABS. *See* acrylonitrile-butadiene-styrene
acetate fiber **6:** 21; **7:** 36, 46
acetate film **1:** 47
acetic acid **1:** 37, 55
acid rain **8:** 57; **9:** 21, 46, 47
acidic water **8:** 6, 7, 46, 48, 52, 57
acids **1:** 15; **2:** 28, 30; **8:** 6, 46, 47, 48, 52, 56, 57
acrylic **1:** 38, 39, 40, 41
acrylic adhesives **6:** 50
acrylic fiber **1:** 39; **6:** 20, 21; **7:** 33, 36, 37, 38, 44, 45, 57
acrylic paints and stains **1:** 41; **6:** 32, 34, 35
acrylic plastics **1:** 38-41
acrylic powders **6:** 40
acrylonitrile-butadiene-styrene (ABS) **1:** 38
addition polymers/addition polymerization **1:** 10, 11, 27, 43; **7:** 15
additives **1:** 15, 16, 17; **3:** 51
adhesion **6:** 44, 45, 46
adhesives **1:** 22, 37, 40, 41, 42, 44, 53, 55; **3:** 8, 24, 43, 44, 45, 47, 50, 53, 54; **4:** 35, 41; **5:** 54; **6:** 4, 41-57

adhesive tapes **6:** 54, 57
admiralty brass **2:** 24
adobe **4:** 10, 11
advanced ceramics **4:** 42-57
aggregate **4:** 39, 41
air **9:** 4 AND THROUGHOUT
air bags **9:** 42
air brakes **9:** 35
air conditioning **9:** 26, 52
aircraft **2:** 21, 26, 27, 35, 51; **9:** 29, 32, 34, 35
air cushions **9:** 34-35
air drying **3:** 36
air gun **9:** 35
air in transportation **9:** 32
air pollution **9:** 19, 38-40, 44, 46-47
air pressure **9:** 5, 6, 28, 32, 37
albumen **6:** 49
alcohols **8:** 45, 51
alizarin **6:** 12, 13, 14
alkalis **1:** 15; **2:** 28, 30; **8:** 52
alkyd-based paint **6:** 31, 33
alkyd-based varnishes **6:** 37
alloys, alloying **1:** 15; **2:** 6, 13, 22, 23-27, 28, 34, 35, 37, 42; **4:** 46
alum **3:** 53; **6:** 10
alumina **4:** 38, 46, 50, 51, 54, 56, 57; **5:** 8, 9, 10, 13, 18, 52
aluminosilicates **4:** 14
aluminum **2:** 4, 5, 9, 10, 18, 19, 20, 21, 23, 24, 26, 27, 29, 30, 32, 50, 53; **4:** 14, 36
aluminum oxide **4:** 46, 50, 57; **5:** 13
amalgams **4:** 55
amides **7:** 10, 47
ammonia **9:** 41
amorphous solid **5:** 5, 15
amphibious vehicles **9:** 33
anaerobics **6:** 50
ancient glass **5:** 29
angle of incidence **5:** 20
aniline dyes **6:** 14, 22; **7:** 38
aniline mauve **6:** 14
animal glue **6:** 49
anions **8:** 10
annealing **5:** 50
anodized duralumin **2:** 32
anodizing **2:** 27, 32
antimony **2:** 45
antirust paint **6:** 33
anvil **2:** 12, 20
aqueous solutions **8:** 43, 44, 46
Araldite® **1:** 55
aramids **7:** 36, 50, 51
Archimedes' principle **8:** 38
argon **9:** 18, 36, 54, 55
armor **2:** 42, 43
armor plating **2:** 42
Arnel® **1:** 47; **7:** 46
arsenic oxide **5:** 11
artifacts **4:** 12
artificial dyes **6:** 7
artificial fibers **3:** 50; **7:** 7, 8, 9, 10, 12, 15, 16, 17, 19, 24, 30, 31, 32-57
artificial polymers **7:** 12
aspen **3:** 15
atmosphere **9:** 12, 14, 18, 20-21, 43, 44, 54, 55
atmospheric pressure **8:** 21, 22, 28; **9:** 6. *See also* air pressure
atomizer **9:** 28

atoms **2:** 6, 8, 9, 22, 23; **4:** 5, 9; **5:** 4, 5, 39; **7:** 4, 9; **8:** 8; **9:** 8, 10
atoms, properties in plastics **1:** 13
ax **3:** 6
azo dyes and pigments **6:** 7, 10; **7:** 38

B

backbone chain **1:** 27, 43, 55; **7:** 4. *See also* polymers
backbone unit **1:** 54. *See also* monomers
bagasse **3:** 49
Bakelite **1:** 43
balloons **9:** 8, 14, 51, 54
balsa **3:** 17, 20, 23
bamboo **3:** 49
band saw **3:** 34
barbed wire **2:** 6, 30, 31
barium carbonate **4:** 46; **5:** 9
barium titanate **4:** 46
bark **3:** 4, 6, 13, 14, 32
barometer **8:** 28
base metal **2:** 23, 24
bast fibers **7:** 20
batch kiln **4:** 19, 28
batch processing **7:** 32
batik **6:** 19
bauxite **4:** 38
beating metals **2:** 22-23
beech **3:** 17, 18, 23
bellows **9:** 28
bells **2:** 14, 44
bending ceramics **4:** 9
bending metals **2:** 12, 22, 35, 51
bends, the **9:** 42
benzene **1:** 33, 39
benzene ring **1:** 10; **6:** 15
Bessemer converter **2:** 46
Bessemer, Henry **2:** 47
binder **4:** 55; **6:** 27, 39
bioceramics **4:** 54-56
blacksmith **2:** 12, 22, 41
blast furnace **2:** 47
bleaches **6:** 24, 26
bleaching paper **3:** 52, 57
blending fibers **7:** 12, 25, 41, 43, 44, 45
blends, blending ceramics **4:** 17, 22, 36, 38
blood **8:** 6, 48
blood glue **6:** 49
bloom **2:** 40
blow molding **1:** 19
blown glass **5:** 32-33
board **3:** 34, 36, 42, 43, 44, 45, 46
bobbin **7:** 25, 42
boil, boiling water **8:** 11, 16, 20, 48
boilers **8:** 21, 22, 32, 33, 54
boiling point of water 11, 19, 20, 49, 48, 54
boll, boll fiber **7:** 4, 20, 25
bond paper **3:** 55
bonds and bonding **2:** 6, 7; **4:** 4, 5, 6, 9, 15, 25; **8:** 8, 9, 11, 14. *See also* covalent bonding, hydrogen bonds and bonding, ionic bonding
bone china **4:** 25
book paper **3:** 55
borax **5:** 13
boric oxide **5:** 8, 13
borosilicate glass **5:** 12, 13, 19
bottles **5:** 10, 28, 30, 43, 46-47
Boyle's law **9:** 8, 9
brass **2:** 6, 16, 24, 34, 41, 44

brazilwood **6**: 12
brick **8**: 26, 27, 28
brick colors **4**: 15, 16, 27, 29
bricks and brick making **4**: 4, 10, 14, 15, 16, 17, 19, 26-31, 32, 33, 34, 39
brighteners, for fabric and paper **6**: 24
brine **8**: 41, 47, 50, 51
bristles **7**: 6, 48
brittleness in materials **2**: 4, 8, 14, 17, 18, 41; **3**: 19; **4**: 8-9; **5**: 5, 23
broad-leaved trees **3**: 17
bronze **2**: 15, 25, 37, 38, 39, 40, 41, 43, 44, 45, 55
Bronze Age **2**: 14, 37-38, 40, 41, 55
buildings, use of metals in **2**: 18, 28, 31, 49, 54-57
bull's-eye glass **5**: 39
bulletproof glass **5**: 26
bulletproof vests **7**: 8, 14, 34, 51
bullets **2**: 42, 45
buoyancy **8**: 38-39
burlap **7**: 11
burn **3**: 27, 28
burning plastics **1**: 12, 13, 14, 25
butadiene rubber **1**: 42
butene **1**: 28

C

cadmium **2**: 10, 30
calcium **2**: 5, 10; **4**: 15, 36, 53
calcium halophosphate **4**: 52
calcium oxide **4**: 37, 38; **5**: 8
calcium silicate **4**: 52
calcium sulfate **4**: 34
calcium tungstate **4**: 52
calorific value of wood **3**: 28
cambium **3**: 10, 12, 13, 14
cannons **2**: 15, 25, 44, 45
canoes **1**: 53; **3**: 6
canvas **7**: 11
capacitors **4**: 7, 44, 46-47; **5**: 18
capillarity **8**: 26-28
capillary action **6**: 54
car industry **2**: 49, 52
carbohydrates **7**: 10
carbon **1**: 4, 6, 7, 10, 13, 16, 27, 28, 39, 41, 42, 43, 54, 55, 57; **2**: 10, 23, 39, 41; **6**: 4; **7**: 4, 7, 8, 14, 49, 50, 53, 55, 56; **9**: 21, 48, 49
carbon black **1**: 42; **6**: 9, 29
carbon chains **1**: 7, 13, 27
carbon compounds **1**: 4; **6**: 9
carbon cycle **9**: 48, 49
carbon dioxide **9**: 11, 19, 36, 43, 48-50, 51
carbon fiber **4**: 57; **7**: 56-57
carbonic acid **8**: 48
cardboard **3**: 46, 56
carding **7**: 25
carmine **6**: 12, 13, 14
carpets **7**: 24, 25, 27, 33, 43, 44, 45, 48, 49
carving **3**: 9, 22
casein **6**: 49
cashmere **7**: 27
cassiterite **2**: 38
cast bronze **2**: 15, 45
cast glass **5**: 30
casting **2**: 13, 14-17, 18, 25, 38, 39, 44; **4**: 17, 18, 43
cast iron **2**: 40, 41, 45, 49, 54, 55, 56, 57
catalysts **7**: 15, 42; **8**: 7; **9**: 10, 41

catalytic converters **2**: 11; **4**: 43, 53, 57; **9**: 39, 40
cations **4**: 6, 15; **8**: 10
cedar **3**: 16
Celanese® **7**: 46
cellophane **1**: 47
celluloid **1**: 7, 46
cellulose **1**: 44, 46, 47, 49; **3**: 10, 46, 47, 48, 50, 51, 52; **7**: 10, 11, 12, 13, 25, 31, 39, 40, 41, 46
cellulose diacetate **1**: 47
cement **4**: 10, 13, 35-37, 38, 39, 40, 41. *See also* dental cement
central heating systems **2**: 56; **8**: 32, 33; **9**: 25, 26, 27
ceramic **4**: 4 AND THROUGHOUT
ceramic capacitors **4**: 46-47
ceramic electrical insulators **3**: 28; **9**: 22
ceramic molds **1**: 9
ceramics **1**: 15, 16; **2**: 4, 12, 49; **5**: 4, 5, 14
ceramics used in nuclear reactors **4**: 54
ceramic tiles. *See* tiles
CFCs. *See* chlorofluorocarbons
chain mail **2**: 42
chalcogenide glasses **5**: 15
change of state **8**: 5, 16-20, 21, 22; **9**: 52
charcoal **2**: 38, 39, 40, 41, 46, 47
Charles's law **9**: 9
charring **7**: 7, 10, 15, 17, 24, 33, 39, 44, 57
checks **3**: 20
chemical properties of glass **5**: 16-18
chewing gum **1**: 8
chicle **1**: 8
china **4**: 25
china clay **3**: 51, 54; **4**: 14, 16, 24, 25; **6**: 9
chipboard, chipwood **1**: 22; **3**: 34, 42, 43, 44
chips, chippings **3**: 11, 32, 34, 50
chlorine **1**: 10, 29, 39; **3**: 52
chloroethylene **1**: 10
chlorofluorocarbons (CFCs) **9**: 44
chromium **2**: 10, 25, 28, 30; **5**: 11, 21
chromium plating **2**: 30, 34
circular saw **3**: 34
clay minerals **4**: 14
clays **4**: 4, 9, 10, 14, 15, 17, 18, 28
clay suspensions **4**: 17, 18
clearcut tree felling **3**: 32
cling wrap **1**: 11
clothing **7**: 8, 16, 29, 33, 39, 41, 43, 44, 45
clouds and cloud formation **8**: 4, 7; **9**: 3, 9, 20, 52, 53
coal **2**: 47, 49; **9**: 48, 49
coal tar **6**: 7, 8, 10, 16
coated papers **3**: 55
cobalt **2**: 9; **5**: 11, 21
cobalt aluminate **4**: 51
cobalt oxide **5**: 11
cobalt silicate **4**: 51
cochineal **6**: 12, 13
coins **2**: 20, 26, 38, 39
coir **7**: 11
coke **2**: 47
cold bending **2**: 35
cold forging **2**: 20, 23
cold rolling **2**: 18
cold-working metals **2**: 14
collecting gases **9**: 10
colorants **1**: 15, 16; **6**: 6, 9, 10, 24, 25, 26

colored glass **5**: 21, 33-35
colorfast **6**: 8; **7**: 52
coloring glass **5**: 11
coloring paper **3**: 54
color mixing **6**: 4-6
composite materials **7**: 56, 57
composite wood **3**: 24
compounds of metals **2**: 4, 6; **9**: 36, 38, 43, 47, 48
compressed air **9**: 14, 28-31, 34, 35, 54
compressibility of water **8**: 31
compression molding **1**: 18
compression resistance in ceramics **4**: 8
concrete **4**: 10, 35, 39-41
condensation **8**: 16, 18-19, 49, 50; **9**: 16, 53
condensation polymer, condensation polymerization **1**: 43; **7**: 10, 14
conductivity. *See* electrical conductivity and heat (thermal) conductivity
conifers, coniferous trees **3**: 16, 48
contact adhesives **6**: 41, 52-53
contact lenses **1**: 40
continuous casting **2**: 17
continuous production tunnel kilns **4**: 30
convection **9**: 18, 22, 25, 27. *See also* heat convection
cooling towers **8**: 34
copolymer **1**: 38
copper **2**: 4, 5, 6, 9, 10, 14, 16, 17, 23, 24, 25, 26, 27, 28, 30, 36, 37, 38, 39, 40, 41, 43, 45, 53, 56; **4**: 47; **5**: 11
copper ore **2**: 5
copper oxide **5**: 11
cores **5**: 30, 31
corn glue **6**: 49
Corning Corporation **5**: 13
corrosion **2**: 28, 32; **8**: 27, 53, 54, 57
corrosion in glass **5**: 13, 14, 16, 17, 18
corrosion in water **8**: 53-54
corrosion resistance **1**: 29, 30, 43; **2**: 23, 24, 25, 26, 27, 28-34, 38, 49, 51; **4**: 32, 46, 54, 55, 57
corrugated iron **2**: 31
cotton **1**: 13, 51; **3**: 49, 55; **7**: 4, 7, 17, 19, 20, 21, 25, 43
covalent bonding **4**: 5; **8**: 8, 9
crankshaft **8**: 22
crease-resistant fabrics **7**: 17, 27, 42, 46. *See also* durable-, permanent-, and stay-pressed fabrics
creosote **3**: 24, 40; **6**: 36
creping **3**: 56
crimped materials **7**: 27, 37; **8**: 26
cristallo **5**: 37
critical angle **5**: 20
crockery **4**: 19, 24
cross linking **7**: 17
crown glass **5**: 39, 49
crucible glass **5**: 29-30
crucibles **2**: 47; **4**: 32
crude oil **1**: 6, 28; **6**: 7, 8, 10, 16, 26, 36; **9**: 45
crysocolla **2**: 5
crystal glass **5**: 37
Crystal Palace **2**: 56; **5**: 42
crystals and crystalline materials **2**: 3, 6, 13, 14, 18, 22; **4**: 6-8, 9, 19, 34, 35, 39, 43, 48, 50, 52; **5**: 4, 6, 14
cullet **5**: 42
curing concrete **4**: 39

curing rubber **1:** 9
cut glass **5:** 9
cutlery **2:** 31
cyanoacrylate **1:** 40; **6:** 50, 54
cylinder glass **5:** 40
cylinders **8:** 21, 22

D

Dacron® **1:** 50; **7:** 42
daggers **2:** 41
Dalton, John **9:** 11
Dalton's law **9:** 10
Damascus steel **2:** 41
damp-proof layer **8:** 28
Darby, Abraham 47
debarking machine **3:** 34
decay in wood **3:** 24, 30, 41, 43
deciduous trees **3:** 30
decolorizing glass **5:** 11, 36
decompose **7:** 7, 10, 14, 24, 33, 44
decomposition of plastics **1:** 24, 49
decomposition of water **8:** 17, 56
decompression sickness **9:** 42
decorative laminates **1:** 22
defibering **3:** 53
density of gases **9:** 9, 15
density of plastics **1:** 4, 24, 29, 32, 33
density of water **8:** 8, 12, 13, 20, 28, 37, 39
density of wood **3:** 20-24, 27
dental cement **4:** 55-56
dental fillings **4:** 3, 55
desalination **8:** 41, 50-51
desalting **8:** 41. *See also* desalination
detergents **8:** 29, 30-31, 46, 55
deuterium **8:** 14
diamond **4:** 4, 6, 57
die casting **2:** 17
die extrusion **1:** 17, 18; **2:** 19
diene plastics **1:** 42, 43
dies **2:** 17, 19, 21, 39; **4:** 17, 28, 57
diffusion **8:** 39, 40; **9:** 17
dipping **1:** 21
direct dyeing **7:** 30
dishwasher-proof plastic containers **1:** 32
disperse dyeing **6:** 21-22
disposable plastics **1:** 14, 20, 23, 24, 33, 47, 51
dissociation in water **8:** 16, 47, 55(gloss)
dissolving substances in water **8:** 6, 42-57
distillation of air **9:** 36
distillation of water **8:** 49-51
distilled water **8:** 49, 50
doped ceramics **4:** 8, 45, 51, 52, 53
doping **4:** 6, 45
double glazing **5:** 26; **9:** 23
Douglas fir **3:** 16, 20
drafts **9:** 27
drawing **2:** 13, 19
drawing dies **2:** 19; **4:** 57
drawing fibers. *See* stretching fibers
drinking water supplies **8:** 6
drip-dry fabrics **1:** 47
dry cleaned **7:** 41
dry felting **3:** 45
dry ice **9:** 50
drying wood **3:** 23, 36, 37
dry-press process **4:** 28
dry spinning **7:** 34
ductile material **2:** 18
Dumas, Jean-Baptiste-André **5:** 38

durable-press fabrics **7:** 16-17. *See also* permanent- and stay-pressed fabrics
dyeing artificial fibers **7:** 37
dyeing metals **2:** 32
dyeing natural fibers **6:** 7, 17, 18, 20, 21, 24; **7:** 30
dyeing plastics **1:** 16, 39
dyeing synthetic fibers **6:** 17, 20, 21
dyes **6:** 4-26; **7:** 7, 30, 38
dyes and dyeing fibers **6:** 6, 7, 17, 21, 22, 23, 24; **7:** 7, 24, 25, 27, 29, 30, 37, 38, 41, 42, 45, 46, 47, 51, 52
dyes and papermaking **3:** 51, 54

E

early wood **3:** 14
earthenware **4:** 22, 23, 24, 25
eggshell paint **6:** 34
Egypt **5:** 28, 33
Egyptians **5:** 30
Eiffel Tower **2:** 54
eighteen-carat gold **2:** 26
elastic limit **2:** 20, 35
elasticity in materials **1:** 8, 56, 57; **2:** 20, 22, 35; **5:** 23; **7:** 4, 7, 37, 47, 57; **9:** 14, 28
elastic properties of wood **3:** 8, 19, 29
electrical conductivity **1:** 4, 13, 14; **2:** 4, 6, 9, 11, 25, 53; **4:** 4, 6, 7, 8, 45, 46, 52-53, 56; **5:** 15, 18 ; **7:** 56, 57; **8:** 10, 44, 46-48; **9:** 21, 22
electrical insulation **1:** 13, 14, 29, 32, 35, 37, 44, 45; **3:** 28; **4:** 7, 22, 44, 46, 52, 56; **5:** 18; **8:** 46, 47; **9:** 21-22
electrical properties of glass **5:** 18
electrical transformers **2:** 10
electric arc furnace **2:** 49
electric arc welding **2:** 52
electrofloat process **5:** 50
electrolysis **8:** 47, 56
electrolytes **8:** 46, 48
electromagnet **2:** 9
electronics **4:** 44-45, 46, 52, 53
electrons **1:** 13; **2:** 6, 7, 9, 28, 30; **4:** 5, 7, 47, 52; **8:** 9, 47, 56
elements **2:** 4, 8; **8:** 4; **9:** 4. *See also* heating elements
Empire State Building **2:** 57
emulsion paints **6:** 33, 34
enamel paints **2:** 33; **6:** 38
enamels, enameling **2:** 24, 33, 49, 57; **4:** 23; **5:** 14; **6:** 38
energy **8:** 14, 16, 17, 23, 35
energy efficient glasses **5:** 15
engineered wood products **3:** 42
epoxy, epoxy resin **1:** 53, 54, 55
epoxy resin adhesives **6:** 50-51
epoxy resin varnishes **6:** 37
etching glass **5:** 17
ethylene **1:** 10, 17, 20, 28, 33, 35, 37, 41
ethylene-propylene **1:** 32
eucalyptus **3:** 15
evaporation **8:** 4, 6, 16, 18-19, 20, 42
exosphere **9:** 20
exothermic reaction **8:** 52
expansion properties of glass **5:** 19
external combustion engine **8:** 22
extrusion **1:** 17, 19; **2:** 13, 19; **7:** 4, 10, 14, 32, 33, 34, 36, 37, 38, 42, 45, 46
eyeglasses **1:** 20; **5:** 26, 55

F

fabrics **1:** 13, 31, 44, 45, 47; **7:** 8, 10, 12, 15, 19, 20, 22, 25, 33
fat **8:** 30, 45, 46, 52
feldspars **4:** 15, 17, 22, 26, 29
felt **3:** 51
felting **3:** 45, 46; **7:** 28
ferric oxide **5:** 11
ferrites **4:** 48, 49
ferromagnetic metals **2:** 10
ferrous oxide **5:** 11
fertilizers **8:** 6; **9:** 36, 38, 41
fiberboard **3:** 45
fiberglass **1:** 16, 23; **2:** 12; **5:** 54, 57; **7:** 6, 54; **9:** 23. *See also* glass fiber
fibers **1:** 7, 18, 23, 25, 31, 39, 44, 46, 47, 48, 50, 51, 56; **3:** 4, 18, 22, 23, 24, 26, 28, 45, 46; **6:** 6, 17, 22, 23, 24; **7:** 4 AND THROUGHOUT; **9:** 23, 42
fibers in papermaking **3:** 4, 46-57
fibrin **7:** 28
filaments **6:** 41; **7:** 4, 28, 32, 33, 34, 47
filler **3:** 54; **4:** 15, 29, 30, 33, 39, 55; **6:** 9
finishes on paper **3:** 53-54
fir **3:** 16, 20
fire extinguishers **8:** 36, 37; **9:** 50
fire resistance **1:** 12, 14, 38, 46, 48, 52; **7:** 8, 14, 34, 45, 54
firing bricks **4:** 28-29, 30-31
firing ceramics **4:** 18-19, 20, 28, 29, 30, 31, 46
firing temperature **4:** 20, 30
fishing line **1:** 48, 49; **7:** 49, 54
flak jacket **2:** 42
flame-resistance in wood **3:** 27
flash distillation **8:** 50-51
flat glass **5:** 33, 34, 39, 40, 42, 49-52, 53
flat paint **6:** 34
flax **3:** 49; **7:** 19, 20, 21
fleece **7:** 26
flexibility in fibers **7:** 6, 7
flint **4:** 5
float glass **5:** 49, 50, 51
float glass process **5:** 50-51
floating **8:** 8, 38-39, 51
fluorescent lamps and tubes **4:** 51, 52; **9:** 55, 56
fluorine **1:** 10, 41
fluorite **4:** 50
fluxes **2:** 40; **4:** 15, 16, 27, 29; **5:** 8, 9, 16
foamed polystyrene **1:** 14, 23, 32, 34
foaming agents **1:** 21; **8:** 37
foams and foamed plastics **1:** 14, 21-22, 23, 32, 33, 34, 56, 57
food coloring **6:** 24, 25-26
forests **3:** 10, 17, 30, 31, 32, 56
forging **2:** 13, 20, 23 41
former **5:** 8
Formica® **1:** 44
forming bricks **4:** 17, 28, 29
fossil fuels **9:** 38, 47, 48, 49
fractional distillation **9:** 36
fracturing in ceramics **4:** 5, 8, 9
fracturing in glass **5:** 6, 12, 13, 24
frame for construction **3:** 5, 7, 38, 44
freeze-dried ceramics **4:** 43
freeze-dry food **9:** 41
freezing **8:** 16, 17
freezing point of water **8:** 8, 31, 49, 50
fresh water **8:** 6
frit **5:** 52; **6:** 39

froth flotation **8:** 51
froth separation **8:** 51
fuel, wood **3:** 5, 6, 28
fumes **1:** 14, 25
furnaces **2:** 12, 41. *See also* glass furnaces
furniture **1:** 14, 22; **3:** 5, 17, 19, 22, 32, 36, 42, 43
fuses **2:** 26
fusing ceramics **4:** 9, 19, 20, 24, 30

G

galvanic protection **2:** 30-32
galvanized iron **2:** 57
galvanized steel **1:** 13;l **2:** 30, 31
galvanizing **2:** 6, 31
gang saw **3:** 34
gaseous state of water. *See* water vapor
gases **8:** 4, 5, 6, 7, 16, 17, 24, 42, 47, 56, 57; **9:** 4 AND THROUGHOUT
gas laws **9:** 8-10
gas-proof plastics **1:** 37, 51
gears **2:** 21
gelatin **6:** 48
gel spinning **7:** 34, 36
giant molecules **7:** 4
gilding metals **2:** 24
ginning **7:** 25
glass **1:** 12, 13, 23, 38, 40, 44, 52; **2:** 4, 33, 50, 56; **4:** 9, 19, 20, 21, 22, 25, 26, 30, 32, 40; **5:** 4 AND THROUGHOUT; **6:** 38
glass adhesives **6:** 55
glass beads **6:** 39
glass blowing **5:** 33
glass ceramics **4:** 53; **5:** 14, 19
glass enamel **2:** 33; **6:** 38
glass fiber **1:** 16, 22, 23, 53; **4:** 57; **7:** 6, 53-54, 55, 56; **5:** 13, 54
glass furnaces **5:** 14, 29, 32, 36, 41, 42, 43, 50, 55
glassmaker's soap **5:** 36
glass microfiber **7:** 6
glass powder **6:** 38, 39
glass transition temperature **7:** 44
glassy state **5:** 5
glazes and glazing **4:** 9, 20-21, 22, 23, 24, 25, 29, 31, 51; **5:** 13, 14, 24; **6:** 38
global warming **9:** 49
gloss paint **6:** 29, 31, 33, 34, 35
glucose **3:** 10; **7:** 12
glue **6:** 10, 41, 48-49
glulam **3:** 42
gobs **5:** 32, 43
gold **2:** 4, 5, 9, 10, 11, 25, 26, 28, 36, 37, 39, 40; **8:** 55
Golden Gate Bridge **2:** 56-57
gold nuggets **2:** 36, 37
Goop **6:** 56
grain, in wood **3:** 9, 16, 17, 18, 24
graphite **4:** 4, 6, 7, 57
gravity **8:** 25, 32; **9:** 14
greaseproof paper **3:** 56
Greece **5:** 28
Greeks **2:** 42, 43; **4:** 13, 35; **8:** 4
greenhouse effect **9:** 21, 49, 50
ground glass **5:** 17, 36, 49, 56
groundwater **8:** 7, 55
growth rings **3:** 13, 14, 16, 20
gum arabic **6:** 49
gums **3:** 10, 12, 13, 14, 20, 22, 27, 46, 54; **6:** 49; **7:** 19, 20

gunmetal **2:** 25
gypsum **4:** 34, 37, 38

H

hairs **7:** 6, 7, 9, 10, 21, 22, 25, 26, 27
Hall, Charles M. **2:** 50
hammering metals **2:** 20, 37, 39, 40, 41, 43
hard water **8:** 55
hardness in metals **2:** 8
hardwoods **3:** 16, 17, 18, 19, 22, 23, 28, 48
harvesting trees **3:** 30-32
HDPE. *See* high-density polyethylene
headsaw **3:** 34, 36
heartwood **3:** 12, 13, 14
heat—effect on plastics **1:** 4, 11, 12, 13, 14, 21, 24, 25, 35, 37, 43, 44, 48, 52
heating elements **4:** 52, 53; **8:** 38, 55
heating metals **2:** 12, 13, 20, 21, 22-23, 26, 40, 41
heat (thermal) conductivity **1:** 14; **2:** 4, 6, 9, 33; **4:** 4; **5:** 7, 12, 19; **8:** 32-35, 37; **9:** 15, 22, 26, 27
heat (thermal) insulation **1:** 14, 21, 23, 34, 43, 53, 57; **3:** 8, 27-28, 57; **4:** 42; **5:** 7, 18; **7:** 27, 36, 46, 54; **9:** 22-23
heat capacity **8:** 32. *See also* thermal capacity
heat convection **8:** 37-38; **9:** 25, 27
heat storage **8:** 32-35
heavy water **8:** 14, 15
helium **9:** 18, 54-55
hematite **2:** 5
hemp **7:** 11, 19, 20, 21
Héroult, Paul-Louis-Toussaint **2:** 50
high-density polyethylene (HDPE) **1:** 26, 29, 30, 31, 32
high-k glass **5:** 18
Hindenburg **9:** 51
holograms **5:** 22
hot glue **1:** 42
hot rolling **2:** 18
hotworking **2:** 13, 14
household water systems **8:** 33
hovercrafts **9:** 32-34
human hair **7:** 6
humidity **9:** 21, 26, 52, 53
hydration **4:** 35; **8:** 56
hydraulics and hydraulic action **8:** 31
hydroelectric power generation **8:** 35
hydrofluoric acid etching **5:** 17
hydrogen **8:** 8, 9, 14, 16, 47, 52, 54, 55-56; **9:** 10, 18, 19, 41, 49, 51, 54
hydrogen bonds and bonding **6:** 20; **7:** 17, 39, 51; **8:** 11-13, 14, 36
hydrogen chloride **1:** 35
hydrolysis **7:** 46
hydrophilic substances **8:** 30, 45
hydrophobic substances **8:** 29, 30, 45
hygrometer **9:** 52
hypocaust **9:** 24, 25

I

ice **8:** 8, 11, 12, 13, 16, 17, 24, 25
Illing, Moritz **5:** 53
immiscibility **8:** 28
impermeable ceramics **4:** 20, 22. *See also* watertight ceramics
impurities in water **8:** 7, 48, 49
indigo **6:** 11, 13, 14, 15, 20, 21
indium oxide **4:** 53

Industrial Revolution **2:** 43, 46-49, 54; **4:** 13; **7:** 22; **8:** 21
inert gases **9:** 21, 41, 42, 53, 55
ingrain dyeing **6:** 21, 22; **7:** 38
injection molding **1:** 18, 25, 32, 50
inks **6:** 8, 9
inner bark **3:** 12, 13
inorganic materials **6:** 9
insulation. *See* electrical insulation and heat (thermal) insulation
integrated circuits **4:** 8, 45
International Space Station **5:** 52
ionic bonding **4:** 5
ionic substances **8:** 42, 46
ions **2:** 6, 7; **4:** 6, 7, 8, 15; **8:** 9, 40, 41, 42, 43, 44, 46, 47
iron **2:** 4, 5, 9, 10, 11, 12, 16, 18, 21, 22, 23, 25, 30, 31, 37, 38, 39, 40, 41, 43, 44, 45, 46, 47, 49, 54, 55, 560, 41, 43, 46, 47; **4:** 16, 24, 27, 36, 38, 48; **8:** 53, 54
Iron Age **2:** 38-41
ironed **7:** 33
ironing fibers **7:** 16-17, 33, 41, 44, 49
ironwood **3:** 20
iron ore **2:** 5
iron oxide **2:** 5, 40; **4:** 38, 49; **5:** 8
iron staining **4:** 16, 24, 27
irrigation **8:** 6
isocyanates **6:** 43
isoprene **1:** 6, 8
isotopes **8:** 14
ivory **1:** 46

J

Jesse Littleton **5:** 13
jewelry **2:** 24, 25, 26, 36, 37, 39, 50
jiggering **4:** 25
jute **7:** 19, 20

K

kaolin, kaolinite **3:** 54; **4:** 14, 16, 24, 25
kapok **7:** 20
keratin **7:** 26
Kevlar® **1:** 48; **2:** 42; **7:** 8, 34, 50, 51
kiln drying of wood **3:** 36, 37
kilns **4:** 9, 19, 27, 32, 35, 37, 38, 51; **5:** 14, 38
kinetic energy **8:** 35
knapping **5:** 7
knitting **7:** 22, 23
knots **3:** 18, 20, 26
kraft process **3:** 51, 52
krypton **9:** 18, 54, 56

L

lacquers **1:** 11, 53; **2:** 29; **6:** 40, 42
laminated glass **5:** 21, 26, 27, 28
laminated windshields and safety glass **1:** 23, 37, 37
laminates **1:** 22, 23, 44; **3:** 24 **6:** 50
lanolin **7:** 26
lasers **4:** 52; **5:** 57
latent heat **8:** 17
latent heat **9:** 16, 52
late wood **3:** 14
latex **1:** 8; **3:** 54; **6:** 29, 49
latex paints **6:** 29, 34-35
lathed glass **5:** 30
lattice **8:** 12, 17
laundry powder **6:** 3, 24

LCDs. *See* liquid crystal displays
LDPE. *See* low-density polyethylene
lead **2:** 10, 11, 24, 25, 40, 42, 43, 44
lead crystal glass **5:** 37
lead monoxide **5:** 11
lead oxide **4:** 53; **5:** 8, 11
lead-silicate glass **5:** 22, 55
leaf fiber **7:** 19
leather **6:** 17
lenses **4:** 50; **5:** 9, 21, 22, 26, 55, 56
Liberty Bell **2:** 14
lift, using air **9:** 32, 34, 35
light bulb filaments **2:** 9, 21, 53
light bulbs **5:** 13, 43, 44-45
lightfast pigments **6:** 9
lignin **3:** 10, 46, 48, 50, 51
lime **4:** 13, 35, 38; **5:** 8, 9, 10, 13, 16, 17, 18, 22, 29, 30, 38
limestone **4:** 35, 36, 37, 38; **5:** 9, 38
linen, linen fibers **3:** 49; **7:** 20, 21
linseed oil **1:** 53; **6:** 28, 37
liquefying gases **9:** 14, 36, 41
liquid crystal displays (LCDs) **4:** 53
liquid oxygen **9:** 36
liquid state of water **8:** 8, 15, 16, 19, 20, 21
liquids **5:** 5; **9:** 5, 12; **8:** 4, 5, 14, 16, 17, 19
lithium **2:** 27, 53
lithium oxide **5:** 9
lodestone **4:** 48
logs **3:** 5, 8, 23, 30, 31, 32, 34, 35, 36, 42
logwood **6:** 12
low-density polyethylene (LDPE) **1:** 26, 27, 28, 29, 30
lubricant **4:** 6, 7, 57
lumber **3:** 34
Lycra® **7:** 52

M

machinability of metal alloys **2:** 23
machine-made glass **5:** 42-57
madder plant **6:** 12, 13
magnesia **5:** 8, 9
magnesium **2:** 5, 10, 25, 26, 27, 32, 50
magnetic ceramics **4:** 48-49
magnetic properties of glass **5:** 15
magnetism in ceramics **4:** 48-49
magnetism in metals **2:** 9-10
magnetite **2:** 9; **4:** 48
magnets **4:** 44, 48
mandrel **5:** 53
manganese **5:** 11, 21
man-made fibers **7:** 12, 31
maple **3:** 27
marine ply **3:** 43
Martin, Pierre and Émile **2:** 47
massicot **6:** 12
matting of fibers **7:** 21, 28
mechanical properties of glass **5:** 22-24
medicines **8:** 48
melamine **1:** 22, 45, 53; **6:** 29, 40
melamine-formaldehyde **1:** 22
melting **8:** 8, 11, 12, 14, 16, 17, 49
melting point of water **8:** 11, 49
melting points of metals **2:** 6
melt spinning **7:** 34, 36
mercuric oxide decomposition **9:** 12
mercury **2:** 10, 43
mesosphere **9:** 20
metal fatigue **2:** 27, 35
metallic glasses **5:** 15

metalloids **2:** 8
metal ores **2:** 5, 9, 37, 38
metal oxides **4:** 20, 27, 48; **5:** 11
metallurgy **2:** 12
metals **1:** 4, 5, 12, 13, 15, 16, 23, 48, 52, 55, 56, 57; **2:** 4 AND THROUGHOUT; **3:** 6, 8, 26; **4:** 4, 7, 8, 9, 16, 30, 46, 48, 51, 56; **5:** 6, 15; **8:** 53-55
methane **9:** 18
methyl orange **6:** 14
microelectronic circuits **4:** 53
microfiber **5:** 57; **7:** 6, 18, 19, 46
Middle Ages **2:** 39, 43, 44
mild steel **2:** 29, 49
milk glue **6:** 49
millefiori **5:** 33
minerals **4:** 4, 34, 50; **5:** 4. *See also* clay minerals
mineral water **8:** 7
mining **2:** 5
minting **2:** 39
mirrors **5:** 22, 56
mixtures and water **8:** 19, 32, 42, 49
mixtures in metals **2:** 6, 23
mixtures, mixture of gases **9:** 4, 10, 16-17
modacrylic **7:** 36
moderator **8:** 14
moisture in the atmosphere **9:** 52-53
mold, molding **1:** 9, 12, 18, 19, 20, 21
molded glass **5:** 30
molds and molding **2:** 14, 15, 16, 17, 39, 41; **4:** 9, 12, 17, 28, 29, 43; **5:** 30, 43, 44, 46, 48, 54, 55
molecules **8:** 8, 24. *See also* water molecules
molecules and molecular structures **1:** 6, 7, 10, 11, 33; **7:** 4, 8, 9, 10, 12, 13, 14, 17, 30, 32, 34, 37, 44; **9:** 7, 8, 9, 12-14, 15, 16, 17, 18, 37, 44, 53
monomers **1:** 10
mordant **3:** 53; **6:** 7, 10, 12, 20; **7:** 30
mortar **4:** 16, 35, 38, 39
mosaics **4:** 13, 14, 21; **5:** 33
mud **4:** 11
muskets **2:** 45

N

nail manufacture **2:** 56
nail polish **1:** 46
native copper **2:** 37
native gold **2:** 4, 36
native metals **2:** 4, 36
natural adhesives **3:** 46, 51, 53, 54; **6:** 48-49
natural dyes **6:** 7, 11-13
natural fibers **1:** 13; **6:** 7, 17, 18, 20, 21, 24; **7:** 7, 9, 10, 12, 14, 19-30, 31, 32, 34, 36, 38, 44, 46
natural gas **1:** 17, 28; **9:** 48
natural polymers **1:** 6, 7, 8-9; **7:** 10-12, 14
natural resins **3:** 10, 13, 14, 20, 23, 27, 46, 52, 54, 56; **6:** 37
natural rubber **1:** 7, 8-9, 12, 13, 42
natural varnishes **6:** 37
neon **9:** 18, 54, 57
neoprene **1:** 42; **6:** 52
nets **7:** 22, 44, 49
neutrons **2:** 6
newspaper, newsprint papers **3:** 46, 52, 56
nickel **2:** 9, 24, 26, 30; **4:** 47, 48; **5:** 11
nitric oxide **9:** 30

nitrogen cycle **9:** 38
nitrogen dioxide **9:** 13, 19, 21, 39, 40
nitrogen, nitrogen gas **1:** 21; **9:** 18, 36, 37-42
nitrogen oxides (Nox) **9:** 13, 18, 19, 21, 30, 37, 38, 39, 40, 46
nitrous oxide **9:** 18
noble gases **9:** 53-57
nonflammable gases **9:** 54
noniron plastics **1:** 45, 47
nonmetals **2:** 6, 8; **5:** 18
nonstick plastics **1:** 10, 41
Nox. *See* nitrogen oxides
nucleating agent **5:** 14
nylon **1:** 13, 48-49, 50; **6:** 8, 20; **7:** 10, 14, 30, 31, 32–33, 34, 35, 36, 37, 47-51, 52, 57

O

oak **3:** 5, 17, 18, 19, 28
obsidian **5:** 7
oceans, ocean water **8:** 4, 6, 37
oil **8:** 28, 32
oil paint, oil-based paints **6:** 29, 35
oils **3:** 10; **9:** 45, 48, 49, 54. *See also* crude oil
olefin, olefin fibers **7:** 36, 52
opacity in materials **1:** 24, 30, 33; **3:** 51, 54; **5:** 7, 14
open-pit mining **2:** 5
optic fiber casings **1:** 12
optic fibers, optical fibers, optical glass fibers **5:** 56-57; **7:** 55
optical properties of glass **5:** 20
optical switches **4:** 44
optics **4:** 44-45, 50
ores **2:** 5, 9, 37, 38
oriented strand board **3:** 42, 44
Orlon® **1:** 39; **7:** 45
osmosis **8:** 40-41
Otis, Elisha **2:** 57
outer bark **3:** 12
oven glass **5:** 9
ovenware **5:** 12
oxide film, oxide coat **2:** 10, 11, 29, 30, 32
oxodizing agent **8:** 7, 53
oxygen **1:** 13, 35, 37, 43, 53, 54, 55, 57; **2:** 4, 6, 10, 38, 52; **4:** 6, 7, 8, 14, 27, 53; **8:** 4, 7, 8, 9, 10, 14, 37, 42, 46, 53, 55-56; **9:** 10, 11, 12, 18, 19, 20, 21, 36, 38, 39, 41, 43-45, 47, 48, 51, 54, 55
oxygen cycle **9:** 43
ozone **1:** 29, 57; **9:** 19, 20, 21, 44

P

packaging material **1:** 21, 22, 29, 30, 32, 33, 34, 37, 57; **3:** 46, 51, 57
pad-dry dyeing **6:** 22, 23
painting metals **2:** 28, 29, 33
painting wood **3:** 8, 41
paints **1:** 37, 41, 45, 53p; **6:** 4-16, 27-40
palladium **2:** 26; **4:** 46
PAN. *See* polyacrylonitrile
panning **2:** 4
paper **1:** 22, 23, 37, 44, 46; **3:** 4, 11, 34, 46-57; **6:** 9; **7:** 8, 19, 20, 41; **8:** 26, 29
papermaking **3:** 50-54
paper stock **3:** 54
paper towels **3:** 56
paper weight **3:** 46

papier-mâché **6**: 42
papyrus **3**: 46, 47; **6**: 42
Parkesine **1**: 46
particleboard **1**: 44; **3**: 44
paste, flour-based **6**: 42
patina **2**: 28
PC. *See* polycarbonate
PE. *See* polyethylene
periodic table **2**: 8, 50
permanent hardness **8**: 55
permanent magnets **2**: 10
permanent-press fabrics **7**: 16-17, 44. *See also* durable- and stay-pressed fabrics
Perspex® **1**: 38, 39
PET or PETE. *See* polyethylene terephthalate
petrochemicals **1**: 12; **7**: 8
petroleum, petroleum products **1**: 12; **7**: 12, 31, 52
phenolic varnishes **6**: 37
phenols, phenolic resin **1**: 21, 43, 44
phlogiston **9**: 51
Phoenicians **5**: 32
phosphoric acid **5**: 17
phosphors **4**: 51, 52
photochemical smog **9**: 40
photochromic glasses **5**: 22
photosynthesis **9**: 21, 43, 48
piezoelectrics **4**: 47-48
pigments **1**: 16, 24, 30, 37, 53; **3**: 54; **4**: 51; **6**: 6-10, 11, 27, 29, 40; **7**: 38
Pilkington, Alastair **5**: 49
pine **3**: 16, 23, 27
pistols **2**: 45
pistons **8**: 21, 22
pith **3**: 13
planks **3**: 34, 36, 37, 39
plaster **4**: 18, 34
plaster of Paris **4**: 34
plastering **4**: 34
plastic bags **1**: 4, 10, 13, 18, 22, 28, 29
plastic bottles **1**: 4, 15, 19, 20, 24, 25, 26, 29, 30, 31, 32, 50, 51
plastic change **2**: 22, 35
plastic film **1**: 7, 18, 29, 37, 46,47
plasticity **1**: 4
plasticity in ceramics **4**: 8, 28, 29
plasticity in glass **5**: 23
plasticity in wood **3**: 19
plasticizers **1**: 15, 16, 21; **7**: 17
plastic metal **6**: 51
plastics **1**: 4 AND THROUGHOUT; **2**: 4, 12, 14, 33; **3**: 6; **4**: 43, 49, 56; **5**: 26; **6**: 41, 43, 49; **7**: 8, 32; **9**: 41, 50
plastic sheet **1**: 6, 7, 11, 18, 20, 22, 23, 37, 38, 42, 44, 47, 50
plastic wood **6**: 51
plate glass **5**: 41, 49
plating **2**: 30, 32
platinum **2**: 10, 11, 21; **4**: 43, 57; **8**: 55
pleats **7**: 16, 17, 44
Plexiglas® **1**: 38
pliable properties of wood **3**: 19, 22
plows, plowshares **2**: 44, 46
plumbing **2**: 43
plutonium oxides **4**: 54
plywood **1**: 22, 44; **3**: 24, 42, 43
PMMA. *See* polymethyl methacrylate
pneumatic devices **9**: 29-31
pneumatic trough **9**: 10
polar solvent **8**: 43

polarity in water **8**: 9, 10, 11
poles **3**: 33
polish **3**: 8
polishing **5**: 24, 30, 49, 50, 51
pollution **8**: 51, 57. *See also* air pollution
pollution control **2**: 11
polyacrylonitrile (PAN) **7**: 45
polyamides **1**: 48; **7**: 47, 49
polycarbonate (PC) **1**: 13, 52, 53
polychloroethylene **1**: 10
polyester **6**: 21
polyester fiber **1**: 13, 47; **7**: 10, 14, 17, 18, 31, 32, 33, 34, 36, 42-44, 46, 49, 50, 51, 54
polyethers **1**: 13, 22, 50-54
polyethylene (PE) **1**: 4, 10, 11, 20, 21, 22, 26, 27, 28-30, 31, 32; **7**: 33, 52; **8**: 28
polyethylene terephthalate (PETE or PET) **1**: 20, 24, 25, 26, 50-51; **6**: 21; **7**: 32, 37, 42
polyisoprene **1**: 8
polymer industry **1**: 8
polymerization **1**: 10; **7**: 10, 14, 15, 49
polymer membrane **8**: 41
polymers **1**: 6, 7, 10, 13, 14, 15, 16, 27, 28, 37, 38, 41; **3**: 10; **6**: 17, 28, 43, 49; **7**: 9, 10-14, 31, 32, 33
polymethyl methacrylate (PMMA) **1**: 40-41
polypropylene (PP) **1**: 11, 20, 26, 27, 31-33; **7**: 52
polypropylene fibers **7**: 33, 38, 52
polystyrene (PS) **1**: 10, 14, 20, 21, 23, 24, 26, 33-34, 47, 54; **6**: 57
polytetrafluoroethylene (PTFE) **1**: 10, 41
polyurethane adhesives **6**: 50
polyurethane fibers **7**: 52
polyurethanes **1**: 21, 56-57
polyurethane varnishes **6**: 37
polyvinyl acetate (PVA, PVAc) **1**: 37; **6**: 54
polyvinyl acetate (PVA) adhesive **6**: 54-55, 57
polyvinyl acetate (PVA) glue **1**: 37
polyvinyl chloride (PVC) **1**: 10, 13, 14, 15, 16, 20, 21, 25, 26, 35, 36, 37. *See also* vinyl
polyvinylidene (PVDC) **1**: 36, 37
poplar **3**: 17
porcelain **2**: 26, 57; **4**: 22, 25-26, 52, 56
porcelain enamel **4**: 23; **5**: 14
pores **7**: 30
porous ceramics **4**: 18, 30, 31, 40, 55
Portland cement **4**: 35, 37, 38
Portland cement plant **4**: 36-37
Post-it® Notes **6**: 54
posts **3**: 33
potash **5**: 8, 9
potassium **2**: 5, 8, 10
potato glue **6**: 49
potential energy **8**: 35
pottery **4**: 4, 17, 31
powder coatings **6**: 40
powder forming **2**: 13, 21
powder glass **5**: 52
powder paints **6**: 12, 13
powders **4**: 9, 34, 35, 37, 38, 43-44, 46, 48, 49, 50, 51, 52, 55
PP. *See* polypropylene
precipitation **8**: 55, 57
preservatives **3**: 30, 33, 40, 41; **6**: 36
preserving wood **3**: 30, 40-41

pressing **2**: 20
pressure **9**: 5, 8, 12, 13
pressure cooker **8**: 21
pressure of a gas **9**: 8, 9, 14, 15. *See also* air pressure
pressure-sensitive adhesives (PSAs) **6**: 54
pressure-treated wood **3**: 33, 40
primary colors **6**: 4
primers **6**: 28, 30, 33
Prince Rupert's Drop **5**: 10
properties of gases **9**: 12-17
properties of wood **3**: 19-29
propylene **1**: 11, 28
protective clothing **1**: 14, 48
protective coatings **6**: 27-40
proteins **6**: 17, 48, 49; **7**: 4, 10, 26, 28
protons **2**: 6
PS. *See* polystyrene
PSAs. *See* pressure-sensitive adhesives
PTFE. *See* polytetrafluoroethylene
pugging **4**: 28
pulp fibers **3**: 53
pulp, pulp production **3**: 32, 45, 46, 48, 51-54, 56
pumping engine **8**: 21
pumps **9**: 5, 6, 8, 28
pure liquids **8**: 49
pure water **8**: 6, 49
PVA adhesive **6**: 54-55, 57
PVA glue **1**: 37
PVA, PVAc. *See* polyvinyl acetate
PVC. *See* polyvinyl chloride
PVDC. *See* polyvinylidene
Pyrex® **5**: 12, 13

Q
quartzite **5**: 9
quenching **2**: 41

R
radiation **9**: 21, 22, 27
radiators **9**: 26, 27
radioactive water **8**: 14, 15
radiometer **9**: 14
radon **9**: 54, 56
raffia **7**: 19
rags, rag fibers **3**: 49
railroads, railroad stations and tracks **2**: 17, 18, 48, 49, 54
rain, rainwater **8**: 5, 57
rare earths **4**: 51
Ravenscroft, George **5**: 37
rayon **1**: 47, 48, 51; **3**: 50
rayon fiber **7**: 10, 12, 13, 17, 24, 31, 36, 37, 39-41, 57
rays **3**: 12, 14
reactive **9**: 43
reactive dyes **7**: 30
reactivity of metals **2**: 10-11
reactivity of water **8**: 6, 16, 53, 54
reactivity series **2**: 10; **8**: 54
ready-mixed concrete **4**: 39
recycling **1**: 12, 20, 23-26, 51; **3**: 56-57; **4**: 16; **5**: 3, 6, 41, 42
red oak **3**: 18
reducing agent **8**: 7
redwood **3**: 11, 13, 16
refiners **3**: 53
reflective paints **6**: 39
refraction in glass **5**: 20
refractive index of glass **5**: 21, 37, 55, 56

refractory bricks **4:** 31, 32, 33
refractory, refractory materials **4:** 6, 24, 31, 32-33
refrigerants **8:** 33; **9:** 41, 50
regenerated fibers **7:** 12, 31
reinforced concrete **4:** 40
reinforced fiber **4:** 10
reinforcers **1:** 15, 16; **7:** 57
reinforcing plastics **1:** 15, 16, 23, 44
repositionable adhesives **6:** 54
resin enamel **2:** 33; **6:** 38
Resin Identification Code **1:** 25, 26
resins **1:** 6, 11, 16, 22, 44, 53; **2:** 33; **4:** 43, 55, 56; **6:** 27, 37; **7:** 53, 54, 56, 57. *See also* natural resins and synthetic resins
respiration **9:** 12, 43, 48
respositionable adhesives **6:** 54
rifles **2:** 44, 45
rifling **2:** 45
rising damp **8:** 27
rivets **2:** 43, 52
road materials **4:** 41
Robert, Nicolas-Louis **3:** 46
rocks **8:** 4, 5, 6, 7
rocks and metals **2:** 4, 5, 36, 37, 38, 40, 43, 46, 50
rod glass **5:** 53
rolled glass **5:** 10
rolling **2:** 13, 17, 18, 23
rolling mill **2:** 18, 49
rolls of paper **3:** 51
Roman armor **2:** 40, 43
Romans **2:** 38, 40, 41, 42, 43, 55; **4:** 13, 35; **5:** 34, 36, 39, 49; **9:** 25
roof tiles **4:** 10, 16, 21
rope **7:** 19, 20, 22, 44, 48, 49
rosin **3:** 53
rotary saws **3:** 37
rough sawing **3:** 34-36
rubber **1:** 6, 7, 8, 9, 12, 13, 15, 21, 29, 42, 43, 56; **6:** 9, 49, 52; **7:** 37
rubber tree **1:** 8
ruby, synthetic **4:** 52
rugs **6:** 14; **7:** 27
rust **2:** 11, 27, 28, 29, 30; **8:** 53
rust-preventative surface coatings **6:** 28, 29, 30, 33
ruthenium dioxide **4:** 53

S

sacks, sacking **7:** 11, 20, 21
saffron **6:** 13
salt, salts **8:** 4, 5, 6, 7, 19, 40, 41, 42, 43, 44, 45, 46, 47, 48, 50, 55
sand **4:** 10, 12, 13, 15, 16, 17, 22, 29, 33, 36, 38, 39; **5:** 4, 8, 29
sap **3:** 14, 22, 47
sapphire **4:** 50
sapwood **3:** 10, 12, 13, 14
satin paint **6:** 34
saturated air **8:** 18
saturated solutions **8:** 44
sawdust **3:** 34
sawmill **3:** 23, 31, 34-35
sawn timber **3:** 8, 23, 36, 37
sculpting wood **3:** 8, 9
sealants **1:** 55; **6:** 43, 50, 56
seawater **8:** 7, 9, 19, 41, 42, 47, 50
selenium oxide **5:** 11
semiconductors **5:** 15
semigloss paint **6:** 34

semimetals **2:** 8
semipermeable membranes **8:** 40, 41
sensors **4:** 53
sewage **8:** 6, 41, 51
shakes **3:** 20, 26
shales **4:** 15, 28, 29, 30, 38
shaped glass **5:** 54
sheet glass **5:** 10
sheet-metal **2:** 13, 18, 20
shellac **1:** 6
shingles **3:** 8
shot **2:** 45
siding **3:** 7, 22
Siemens, Friedrich **2:** 47
silica **4:** 15, 38, 46, 57; **5:** 8
silica glasses **5:** 8, 9, 52
silicon **1:** 27, 43, 55; **4:** 14, 36, 37
silicon carbide **4:** 57
silicon chips **4:** 4, 6, 42, 45; **9:** 55
silicon dioxide **4:** 5, 38; **5:** 8
silicone-based adhesives and sealants **1:** 53, 55; **6:** 50, 54, 56-57
silk **1:** 6; **6:** 17; **7:** 4, 6, 10, 19, 21, 28-29; **8:** 29
silk cocoons **6:** 41; **7:** 28
silk substitute **7:** 46
silkworm **6:** 41; **7:** 4, 28
silver **2:** 4, 9, 10, 11, 25, 26, 36, 37, 39, 40, 43; **4:** 46; **8:** 55
silver halide **5:** 22
silver oxide **5:** 11
sinter, sintering **2:** 21; **4:** 9, 44
sisal, sisal fibers **3:** 47; **7:** 19
sizing **3:** 51, 53
skateboard wheels **1:** 56, 57
skein **7:** 22
skyscrapers **2:** 56, 57
slag **2:** 24, 40, 41
slip casting **4:** 17
smell **9:** 17
smelting **2:** 38
soap **8:** 30-31, 46, 55
soda **5:** 8, 9, 10, 17, 18, 22, 29, 38
soda-lime glass **5:** 8, 11, 12, 13, 19, 21, 23, 37, 38, 42, 48
sodium **2:** 5, 7, 10
sodium carbonate **5:** 8
sodium nitrate **5:** 11
sodium oxide **5:** 9
soft-mud process **4:** 28
softwoods, softwood forests **3:** 16, 17, 30, 48, 50
solar cells **5:** 52
solder **2:** 25
solidification **8:** 16
solids **5:** 5; **8:** 4, 5, 16, 17, 24; **9:** 5, 12
solubility of substances in water **8:** 45
solutes **8:** 41, 42
solution **8:** 6, 19, 32, 40, 42, 44
solvay process **5:** 38
solvents **1:** 39, 53; **6:** 27, 33, 34, 35, 37, 38, 40, 52, 54, 57; **8:** 6, 10, 41, 42, 43
sound and wood **3:** 8, 29-30
sound insulation **3:** 8, 29, 30
sound in water **8:** 39
sound-proofing **3:** 29
Space Shuttle **4:** 42; **5:** 52; **7:** 57
space suits **7:** 50-51
spandex **1:** 57; **7:** 36, 52
special fibers **7:** 53-57
speciality plastics **1:** 13

spectrum **5:** 20
spinneret **7:** 32, 34, 35, 36, 37, 41, 42, 45, 46, 47
spinning **1:** 7, 25; **7:** 7, 9, 21, 22, 34-36, 37, 40, 41
spinning bobbins **7:** 21
spinning wheels **7:** 21
springwood **3:** 14
spruce **3:** 16
stabilizers **1:** 15, 16; **5:** 8, 9, 13, 16
stained glass **5:** 34
stainless steel **2:** 19, 24, 27, 31, 32, 34
stains, paint **6:** 32, 34, 36
stalactite **8:** 57
stannite **2:** 37
staple **7:** 21, 25, 40
starch glues **3:** 43; **6:** 49
states of matter **5:** 5; **8:** 16
states of water **8:** 16
static electricity buildup **7:** 45, 52
Statue of Liberty **2:** 14, 28
stay-pressed fabrics **1:** 51. *See also* durable- and permanent-press fabrics
stealth technology **4:** 49
steam **8:** 16, 19, 20, 21
steam-driven engines **2:** 47, 49
steam engines **8:** 21-23
steam heating **3:** 22, 36, 43
steam turbines **8:** 23, 34
steel **1:** 7, 13, 15, 48; **2:** 10, 11, 13, 17, 18, 19, 22, 23, 24, 27, 28, 29, 30, 31, 32, 34, 39, 41, 42, 43, 45, 46, 47, 49, 50, 51, 54, 56, 57
sterling silver **2:** 25, 26
stiff-mud process **4:** 28
stone **4:** 4, 12, 26, 35, 39, 41
Stone Age **5:** 7
Stone Age ax **4:** 5
stoneware **4:** 22, 24, 25
straw **3:** 49
strength of metal alloys **2:** 23
strength of wood **3:** 24-26
strengthening glass **5:** 24-27
strengthening, strengthening agents in paper **3:** 48, 49, 54
stretching fibers **7:** 36
strontium carbonate **5:** 9
studding **3:** 38
styrene **1:** 10
styrene-butadiene rubber **1:** 42
styrofoam **1:** 4, 14, 33; **6:** 57
sublimation **8:** 16, 17
subtractive colors **6:** 4
suction pump **9:** 5, 6
sugarcane **3:** 49
suits of armor **2:** 43, 44
sulfur **1:** 13, 27, 29, 43
sulfur dioxide **9:** 19, 46-47
summerwood **3:** 14
super glue **1:** 40, 41; **6:** 54
superconductivity in metals **2:** 9
superconductors **4:** 8, 45
superheated water **8:** 20, 54
surface coating glass **5:** 22
surface coatings **1:** 45, 56; **6:** 4-40
surface tension **8:** 11, 14, 25-26, 28, 37
surfactants **8:** 29
suspensions **8:** 6
sweaters **7:** 27, 44

swords **2:** 36, 40, 41, 42, 43, 44
synthetic adhesives **3:** 43, 44; **6:** 43, 49-50
synthetic ceramics **4:** 48
synthetic dye industry **6:** 15
synthetic dyes **6:** 7, 10, 14, 15, 26; **7:** 38
synthetic fibers **1:** 7, 13, 48, 50; **3:** 50; **7:** 7, 12, 14, 18, 24, 31, 38
synthetic polymers **1:** 6, 7; **7:** 14
synthetic resins **3:** 43, 44
synthetic rubber **1:** 6, 7, 13, 42
synthetics **1:** 7

T

tableware **4:** 16, 24, 25
tangled **7:** 21
tannins **3:** 10
tarmacadam **4:** 41
tarnishing **2:** 10, 11; **5:** 23
teak **3:** 17, 19
Teflon® **1:** 10, 41; **4:** 44
tektites **5:** 7
tempering metals **2:** 23, 41
tempering, tempered glass **5:** 25, 26
temporarily hard water **8:** 55
tensile glass temperature **7:** 17
tensile strength **7:** 7
tension weakness in ceramics **4:** 8
terra cotta **4:** 31
Terylene® **1:** 50; **7:** 33, 42
tetrafluoroethylene **1:** 10
thermal capacity **8:** 34, 36. *See also* heat capacity
thermal properties of glass **5:** 18
thermals **9:** 9
thermistors **4:** 53
thermometers **5:** 12, 53
thermoplastic adhesives **6:** 50
thermoplastic fibers **7:** 44
thermoplastic resins **1:** 11
thermoplastics **1:** 10, 11, 12, 13, 15, 20, 24, 31, 35, 43
thermosets, thermosetting plastics **1:** 11, 12, 13, 20, 22, 23, 24, 43, 44, 46, 57; **6:** 50; **7:** 44
thermosphere **9:** 20
thread **7:** 4, 22, 44, 49
tie dyeing **6:** 19
tiles, ceramic tiles **4:** 10, 16, 17, 21, 23, 24, 25, 26, 31, 42
timber **3:** 4, 34, 36, 38, 39
tin **2:** 8, 10, 24, 25, 26, 30, 37, 38, 40
tin ore **2:** 38
tin oxide **4:** 53
tin plating **2:** 30; **8:** 54
tinting glass **5:** 21
tin-vanadium oxide **4:** 51
tire cord **7:** 37, 41, 44, 49
tires **1:** 8, 42, 51; **9:** 28, 29
titanium **2:** 22, 50, 51, 54
titanium dioxide **4:** 46
toilet tissue **3:** 54
top coat **6:** 28, 30, 31, 34
tortoiseshell **1:** 46
toughened glass **5:** 25
toxic fumes or smoke **1:** 14, 25
transistor **4:** 6, 45
transition metals **2:** 8; **4:** 51
translucent plastics **1:** 12, 13, 30, 53
transparency in materials **1:** 4, 12, 21, 24, 26, 28, 30, 33, 34, 37, 38, 40, 52; **4:** 20, 50, 53; **5:** 4, 6, 15, 19; **6:** 27, 37, 38, 55

tree rings. *See* growth rings
tree trunks **3:** 6, 11, 12, 13, 14, 15, 16, 23, 27, 32, 33
Trevira® **7:** 42
triacetate **7:** 36
Tricel® **1:** 47; **7:** 46
tritium **8:** 14
troposphere **9:** 19, 20
trusses **2:** 54, 55
tube glass **5:** 53
tube metal **2:** 19, 44
tumblers **5:** 48
tungsten **2:** 9, 21, 53
tungsten carbide **4:** 57
tunnel kilns **4:** 19, 25, 28, 30, 31
turpentine **6:** 37
tweeds **7:** 27
twenty-four-carat gold **2:** 26
twine **7:** 11, 22

U

unbleached paper **3:** 56
undercoat **6:** 28, 30, 31, 33
universal solvent **8:** 43
unreactive metals **2:** 4, 8, 11
uPVC. *See* polyvinyl chloride
uranium **5:** 11
uranium oxides **4:** 54
urea **1:** 44
urethane **1:** 53
utility poles **3:** 28

V

V. *See* vinyl and polyvinyl chloride
vacuum **9:** 6, 35, 55
vacuum forming **1:** 19, 20
vacuum pump **9:** 8, 11, 13
valency forces **6:** 45
valve **9:** 6, 7, 28, 31, 39
vapor **8:** 4. *See also* water vapor
vaporize, vaporization **8:** 16
varnishes **1:** 11; **6:** 37, 38
vat dyeing **6:** 20-21
veneers **3:** 9, 18, 42, 43; **6:** 42
Venetian glassmakers **5:** 36
vinyl (V) **1:** 26, 28, 34-38. *See also* polyvinyl chloride
vinyl acetate **1:** 39; **7:** 45
vinyl chloride **1:** 10; **7:** 45
vinyl emulsion **6:** 34
vinyl varnishes **6:** 37
vinyl wallpaper **6:** 47
viscose fiber **1:** 47, 50; **6:** 20; **7:** 36, 39, 40, 41
viscose process **7:** 36, 39-41
viscosity of gases **9:** 13, 15
viscosity of water **8:** 14, 32, 39
vitreous china **7:** 20
vitreous enamel, vitreous enameling **4:** 23; **5:** 13, 14; **5:** 13, 14
vitrify, vitrification **4:** 19-20, 22, 25, 27, 28

W

wallboards **4:** 34
wallpaper adhesive **6:** 47
warping **3:** 19, 24
wash and wear fabrics **7:** 44
waste paper **3:** 56, 57
water **7:** 7, 10, 17, 18; **9:** 4, 5, 16, 21, 22, 27, 30, 46, 47, 48, 53, 54; **8:** 4 AND THROUGHOUT
water-based adhesives **6:** 49, 55, 57

water-based paints **6:** 29, 34-35, 36
water cycle **8:** 4-6
water heaters **8:** 33, 38
water, influence on properties of wood **3:** 20-24, 28
water in papermaking **3:** 50-51
water molecules **8:** 8-13, 44
waterproof fibers **7:** 8, 18, 26, 48
waterproofing **8:** 28-29
waterproof or watertight ceramics **4:** 9, 10, 11, 19, 20, 21, 22, 23, 25, 29
water softeners **8:** 55
water vapor **8:** 4, 6, 16, 17, 19, 20, 49; **9:** 3, 9, 16, 19, 21, 36, 49, 51-53
Watt, James **2:** 56
waxes **3:** 10
wear resistance of metal alloys **2:** 23
weaving **7:** 7, 8, 22, 23
web of paper **3:** 51
welding **1:** 18, 22, 29, 37; **2:** 27, 52
wet felting **3:** 45
wet spinning **7:** 36, 40
wetting **6:** 46-47
wetting agents **8:** 28-29
wet water **8:** 37
white glass **5:** 11, 36
white glue **6:** 54
whitewares **4:** 16, 22-26, 29, 30, 33
windows and window glass **7,** 10, 42, 46, 49, 52
windshields **5:** 21, 23, 26, 27, 54
winning **4:** 28
wire **2:** 19, 31, 53
wire-reinforced glass **5:** 26
woad **6:** 13; **1:** 22, 37, 44, 45; **2:** 12, 15, 36, 40, 44, 46, 47, 48, 55; **3:** 4 AND THROUGHOUT; **5:** 7
wood cells **3:** 10. *See also* cells
wood chips **7:** 12, 38
wooden tiles **3:** 8
wood products in building **3:** 5, 7, 8, 16, 23, 26, 28, 34, 44
wood pulp processing **7:** 31
wool **1:** 13, 39, 51; **3:** 51; **6:** 14, 17; **7:** 6, 10, 19, 21, 26, 43, 45
worsteds **7:** 27
wrought iron **2:** 40, 41, 44, 49, 55

X

xenon **9:** 18, 54, 56

Y

yarn **7:** 22, 25, 28
yew **3:** 16, 17
yttrium vanadate **4:** 52

Z

Zachariasen, W. H. **5:** 39
zinc **2:** 3, 6, 10, 11, 13, 16, 24, 25, 26, 27, 30, 31, 41
zinc coating or plating **2:** 3, 6, 11, 13, 30, 31
zinc oxide **4:** 56; **5:** 9
zircon **4:** 52
zirconia **4:** 4, 53
zirconium dioxide. *See* zirconia
zirconium oxide **5:** 9
zirconium silicate. *See* zircon
zirconium–vanadium oxide **4:** 51